CASSEROLES
Classic to Contemporary

CASSEROLES
Classic to Contemporary

Nina Graybill and Maxine Rapoport

Farragut Publishing Company
Washington, D.C.
1993

PRINTED IN THE UNITED STATES OF AMERICA

Cover illustration by Judy Barczak
Production by Publication Technology Corporation

First printing 1993

Library of Congress Cataloging-in-Publication Data
Graybill, Nina.
Casseroles : classic to contemporary / Nina Graybill and Maxine Rapoport.
    p.   cm.
Includes index.
ISBN 0-918535-15-8 (pbk.) : $11.95

1. Casserole cookery. 2. Cookery, international. I. Rapoport, Maxine. II. Title.
TX693.G73 1993
641.8'21–dc20   92-41354
                                                                                    CIP

For Marlene, who started it all. . .
N.G. and M.R.

*T*hanks to the many friends who so generously shared their ideas and recipes.

Sue Austin

JoAnn Barczak

Sara and Margaux Barczak

Lisa Berger

Catherine Bikk

Carol Bloch

Jean Carper

Anne Clark

Mary Anne Foster

Susan Greer

The Harmans

Karen Menken

Daniel Rapoport

Barry Schweid

Stacey Staniak

Hilary Tuttle

Ellen Vollrath

Mary Ellen Warren

Nahum Waxman

Elizabeth Webber

Al and Kushy Winthrop

Introduction

*C*asseroles. We all eat them, often with undisguised delight. Yet many of us turn up our noses at the word or pretend we never but **never** eat, make, serve or order casseroles.

The truth is, almost everybody, including the food snobs among us, eats—and enjoys—casseroles. Often we do so without realizing it. The creations may be called by other names—arroz con pollo, lasagna, ratatouille, Hungarian paprikash or Hopping John, to name only a few. But these usually ethnic and exotic-sounding dishes are in fact casseroles: one-dish meals slowly cooked in the oven or on the top of the stove, the slow cooking giving the ingredients time to marry and settle into delicious amalgams of flavor and texture. The technique is ancient, the appeal timeless.

Casseroles are especially compatible with today's life styles. For those who work outside the home, a casserole is the perfect dish for advance preparation and easy serving. Most casseroles can be made ahead of time and freeze well. They can be economical, using inexpensive cuts of meat or leftovers, and the quantity can be stretched by adding extra vegetables, pasta or rice.

A tasty casserole, frozen in an ovenproof serving dish, thawed in the refrigerator during the day, then popped into the oven after work, makes an ideal family dinner. Accompany with a green salad, good bread and a simple dessert such as fruit or ice cream. Dinner preparation that night should take you no more than 15 minutes. While your casserole is baking, you can enjoy a glass of wine or help the kids with their homework.

But a casserole—frequently under a pseudonym—can be found just as easily at an elegant dinner party as it can at a family supper. Picture paella served from a silver chafing dish, its glorious colors, aromas and flavors drawing "oohs" and "ahs" from the assembled guests. What better way to celebrate today's return to home entertaining?

We have presented more than 100 casserole recipes, ranging from rich and hearty to elegant to vegetarian to just plain down-home good. Some are old favorites—macaroni and cheese, tuna-noodle casseroles, various chicken and rice or meat and pasta concoctions—modified here and there for variety's sake.

Others reflect the current interest in fresh vegetables, grains and beans and in health-conscious cooking. Try Mixed Grain Casserole or Poached Chicken with Vegetables for a taste of contemporary casserole cookery. We hope you'll find the same satisfaction we do in turning good, wholesome ingredients into even tastier finished products.

All recipes serve six generously. Where possible, we have lightened the fat and calorie content, and we often have used fresh ingredients in place of canned or prepackaged goods. When herbs are called for, use the whole dried variety unless otherwise specified. You can substitute margarine for butter, but the taste won't be quite the same. You can also adjust the amount of salt and pepper to suit your taste. Instant-blending flour, such as Wondra, will be handy for making sauces. Given the great variation in oven thermostats, all baking times are approximate.

Almost any casserole can be prepared in advance. An unbaked casserole, tightly covered, can be refrigerated up to two days. Bring it to room temperature before baking and add 10 to 15 minutes to the cooking time. If you prefer to freeze, cool the completely cooked casserole quickly, wrap in foil or plastic, and store in the coldest part of the freezer; casseroles can be baked frozen but they will take longer to heat. Frozen casseroles in appropriate containers may be thawed in the microwave. If rice or other starch is to be cooked in the pan liquids, you may want to add it after you've thawed the other ingredients and brought them to a boil before finishing the dish in the oven.

No longer need casseroles be the heavy mystery concoctions of yore, but distinctive and delicious one-dish entrees or side dishes you can serve with pride. So welcome back to casseroles and all the good taste and pleasure they bring.

Nina Graybill and Maxine Rapoport

Contents

Pasta, Grains, Vegetables and Legumes

Classic Macaroni and Cheese

*M*acaroni and cheese, like tuna-noodle casseroles, has legions of
admirers. If you've come to rely on the packaged mixes, try this "from
scratch" version for a delightful change.

1 pound medium shells or other short macaroni
4 tablespoons butter
1 pound sharp cheddar cheese, shredded
¼ cup minced parsley
1 tablespoon dry mustard
1 teaspoon salt
¼ teaspoon freshly ground pepper
3 eggs
2 cups milk
½ cup grated Parmesan or Romano cheese

In a large pot, cook macaroni according to package directions until al
dente; drain well and return to pot. Add butter and stir until butter melts.
Add shredded cheese, parsley and seasonings. Mix well.

Pour noodle mixture into a large, shallow glass baking dish. Whisk eggs
and milk together until well combined. Pour over noodles. Top with the
½ cup grated cheese. Bake in a preheated 350-degree oven about 40
minutes until almost set. Remove from oven and let stand 15 minutes
before serving.

Serves 6.

Easy Spinach Lasagna

*B*ack *by popular demand is Spinach Lasagna from our* **Enjoy! Make-Ahead Dinner Party Menus.** *Actually, this is both a healthier version (we have eliminated the eggs and use skim-milk cottage cheese and mozzarella cheese) and an easier version (as we use commercial spaghetti sauce).*

12 lasagna noodles, cooked according to package directions and drained

2 boxes frozen chopped spinach, thawed and squeezed dry

½ cup chopped onions

2 garlic cloves, minced

20 oil-cured black olives, pitted and halved

16-ounce carton skim-milk cottage cheese

¾ cup freshly grated Parmesan cheese, divided

1 teaspoon salt

¼ teaspoon pepper

½ teaspoon thyme

12 ounces part-skim mozzarella cheese, shredded, about 3 cups

1 32-ounce jar spaghetti sauce

½ teaspoon red pepper flakes

In a large mixing bowl, combine the thawed spinach, onions, garlic, olives, cottage cheese, ¼ cup Parmesan cheese, salt, pepper and thyme. Mix the red pepper flakes into spaghetti sauce.

Spread one-third spaghetti sauce in the bottom of a 9 x 13-inch baking dish. Place 4 lasagna noodles over the sauce, then spread with half the spinach-cottage cheese mixture. Sprinkle with half the shredded mozzarella. Repeat layering with one-third spaghetti sauce, 4 lasagna noodles, and remaining spinach-cottage cheese mixture and mozzarella. Top with remaining lasagna noodles and spaghetti sauce and sprinkle with ½ cup Parmesan cheese.

The lasagna can be prepared up to this point, covered and refrigerated 1 day before serving. Remove from the refrigerator 1 hour before baking.

Bake, covered, in a preheated 375-degree oven for 1 hour. Uncover and bake an additional 15 minutes. Let stand 10 minutes before serving.

Serves 6.

Vegetarian Tetrazzini

*A*n attractive side dish or main course with color and flavor.

1 pound fettucini
1 pound mushrooms, cleaned and halved (or quartered if large)
1 large red pepper, diced
1 medium onion, chopped
5 tablespoons butter or margarine
½ cup flour
3 cups milk
1 teaspoon salt
½ teaspoon freshly ground pepper
1 tablespoon dillweed
1 cup grated Parmesan cheese
4 ounces slivered almonds, lightly browned in butter
1 10-ounce box frozen peas
1 tomato, diced, for garnish
½ cup minced parsley, for garnish

Cook fettucini according to package directions until al dente; drain and set aside. If desired, mix with 1 tablespoon oil.

In a large frying pan, saute the mushrooms, red pepper and onion in the butter, in batches if necessary, until mushrooms have given up their liquid and are lightly browned. Return all mushrooms, peppers and onion to pan and sprinkle with the flour; cook, stirring, for several minutes, until smooth. Gradually add the milk, salt, pepper, dillweed and ½ cup of the Parmesan cheese. Cook while stirring until mixture thickens.

Mix the reserved fettucini, almonds and the frozen peas into the vegetables and sauce. Pour into a greased 9 x 13-inch baking dish and sprinkle with the remaining ½ cup of Parmesan.

Bake in a preheated 375-degree oven about 30 minutes, until the casserole is bubbly and cheese is lightly browned. Garnish with diced tomatoes and parsley.

Serves 6.

Herb and Nut-filled Lasagna Roll-ups

This is an interesting variation of a vegetarian lasagna. If a vegetarian meal doesn't appeal to your family or guests, these roll-ups would go well with a platter of well-browned sweet or hot Italian sausages.

12 lasagna noodles, cooked according to package directions and drained
2 tablespoons olive oil
½ cup finely chopped or shredded carrot
½ cup finely chopped celery
½ cup finely chopped onions
1 28-ounce can Italian plum tomatoes, crushed or chopped
1 teaspoon basil, crushed
1 teaspoon oregano, crushed
1 teaspoon salt
¼ teaspoon red pepper flakes
1 cup walnut pieces
¼ cup pine nuts or slivered almonds
½ cup parsley sprigs, long stems removed
¼ cup fresh basil leaves or 2 teaspoons basil, crushed
2 tablespoons olive oil
1 cup low-fat ricotta cheese
¼ cup freshly grated Parmesan cheese
½ teaspoon salt
¼ teaspoon pepper
1 cup shredded mozzarella cheese

Heat the oil in a medium saucepan and saute the carrots, celery and onions until slightly soft. Stir in the tomatoes, basil, oregano, salt and red pepper flakes and bring to a boil; then reduce heat and simmer, uncovered, for 30 minutes. Cool and process in a food processor or blender until smooth, or leave as is if you prefer a chunkier sauce. The sauce can be prepared ahead, covered and refrigerated.

In a food processor fitted with the chopping blade or a blender, process the walnuts, pine nuts, parsley and additional basil until finely chopped. Slowly add the oil through the feed tube and process until smooth.

In a medium bowl, mix together the ricotta cheese, Parmesan cheese, salt and pepper. Add the nut mixture and mix well.

Spread about one-third of the tomato sauce on the bottom of a 9 x 13-inch baking dish. Lay the lasagna noodles on plastic wrap or waxed paper and spread each one with about 1 tablespoon of the nut and cheese mixture. Roll up and place seam side down on the tomato sauce. Pour the remaining sauce over the rolls and cover with aluminum foil.

Bake in a preheated 350-degree oven for 30 minutes. Uncover and sprinkle with mozzarella cheese, then bake uncovered 5 minutes.

Serves 6.

Stuffed Eggplant Rolls on a Bed of Pasta

*H*ere *is a hearty dish that uses eggplant and fettucini, two of our favorite foods.*

½ pound fettucini, cooked al dente, drained and tossed with 1 tablespoon olive oil
2 one-pound eggplants, washed, two sides and both ends sliced off and discarded
Olive oil
Salt and pepper to sprinkle on eggplant
1 tablespoon olive oil
1 tablespoon butter
½ cup minced onion
1 16-ounce can Italian plum tomatoes, drained and pureed in a food processor or blender
1 cup mild salsa
1 teaspoon oregano, crushed
½ teaspoon salt
½ teaspoon chili powder
1½ cups ricotta cheese
¼ cup freshly grated Parmesan cheese
¼ cup thinly sliced green onions
2 tablespoons minced fresh basil, or 2 teaspoons dried basil, crushed
1 tablespoon minced fresh oregano, or 1 teaspoon dried oregano, crushed
2 garlic cloves, minced
½ teaspoon salt
¼ teaspoon pepper
½ cup chopped parsley

Preheat the broiler and rub 2 baking sheets with oil. Cut the eggplants lengthwise into ¼-inch slices. Brush both sides of the eggplant slices with olive oil and sprinkle lightly with salt and pepper. Place on the baking sheets and broil about 3 minutes on each side, or until light brown and somewhat soft. Set aside to cool.

In a medium saucepan, heat the oil and butter and saute the onion until golden. Stir in the tomatoes, salsa, oregano, chili powder and ½ teaspoon salt. Simmer, uncovered, 20 minutes.

While sauce is simmering, mix together in a medium-sized bowl the ricotta, Parmesan, green onions, basil, oregano, garlic, ½ teaspoon salt and ¼ teaspoon pepper.

Spoon a thin layer of the tomato sauce on the bottom of a 9 x 13-inch baking dish. Spread the fettucini over the sauce.

Lay a slice of eggplant on a piece of plastic wrap and spread with about 1½ tablespoons of the ricotta mixture. Roll up from the short end and place seam side down on the fettucini. Repeat with all the eggplant slices.

Spoon the remaining tomato sauce over the eggplant rolls. Cover with a piece of aluminum foil and bake in a preheated 350-degree oven for 40 minutes. Sprinkle with chopped parsley and serve.

Serves 6.

Lasagna with Hearty Meat Sauce

*W*hat *would a casserole cookbook be without a lasagna-with-meat-sauce recipe? We hope you enjoy our version. Don't forget the requisite loaf of crunchy Italian bread.*

12 lasagna noodles, cooked according to package directions and drained
1 pound ground chuck
1 pound sweet Italian sausages, sliced into ½-inch pieces
½ cup chopped onion
2 garlic cloves, minced
½ cup chopped green pepper
½ cup thinly sliced celery
2 tablespoons chili powder
1 28-ounce can Italian plum tomatoes, chopped or crushed
1 teaspoon basil, crushed
½ teaspoon oregano, crushed
½ teaspoon fennel seeds
½ teaspoon salt
2 cups low-fat ricotta cheese
½ cup Parmesan cheese, divided
3 tablespoons chopped parsley
1 egg, beaten
½ teaspoon salt
¼ teaspoon pepper
¼ teaspoon freshly ground nutmeg
12 ounces mozzarella cheese, thinly sliced

In a large skillet, brown the ground chuck, Italian sausage slices, onions, garlic, green pepper and celery. Stir in the chili powder, tomatoes, basil, oregano, fennel seeds and salt. Simmer, uncovered, 30 minutes. The sauce can be prepared, cooled and covered and refrigerated for up to 2 days before assembling the casserole. Reheat the sauce before use.

In a small bowl, mix together the ricotta cheese, 3 tablespoons Parmesan cheese, parsley, beaten egg, salt, pepper and nutmeg.

Spoon in enough tomato sauce to barely cover the bottom of a 9 x 13-inch baking dish. Lay 4 lasagna noodles over the sauce and spread with half the ricotta mixture and half the mozzarella slices. Cover with one third the tomato sauce. Place 4 lasagna noodles on the sauce and repeat the layering. End the layering with 4 lasagna noodles and the remaining tomato sauce; sprinkle with the remaining Parmesan cheese.

Bake, covered, in a preheated 375-degree oven for 45 minutes. Uncover and bake an additional 30 minutes.

Serves 6.

Noodle Kugel with Fruit

This is a casserole that would most often be served as a side dish, possibly with baked or roasted chicken, but it is also a unique entree for the growing numbers of vegetarians.

1 16-ounce package wide egg noodles, cooked as package directs and drained
¼ cup melted butter or margarine
2 eggs, slightly beaten
½ cup sugar
½ teaspoon cinnamon
½ teaspoon ground cardamom
2 crisp apples, cored and chopped
2 pears, peeled, cored and chopped
½ cup fresh orange juice
Juice of ½ lemon
2 teaspoons grated orange rind
½ cup golden raisins
½ cup sliced almonds

In a large bowl, mix noodles with melted butter. With a wooden spoon or rubber spatula, stir in the eggs, sugar, cinnamon, cardamom, chopped apples and pears, orange and lemon juice, orange rind and raisins. The mixture can be covered and refrigerated for several hours or overnight before transferring to the baking dish.

Pour the mixture into a buttered 9 x 13-inch baking dish and bake in a preheated 325-degree oven for 1 hour and 15 minutes. Sprinkle the sliced almonds on top and bake an additional 30 minutes. Let stand for 10 minutes, then cut into squares or rectangles and serve.

Serves 6.

Mixed Vegetables and Rice Casserole

This has been a family favorite for many years, and a favorite of the cook too. In addition to its delicious flavor, it satisfies both the vegetable and carbohydrate components of a meal.

2 cups, about 1 pound, all-purpose potatoes, peeled and cut into 1-inch cubes
2 cups cubed eggplant, about ½ pound
1½ cups cubed zucchini, about ½ pound
1 cup diced green pepper, or combination of green and red peppers
1½ cups chopped onion
2 medium carrots, diced
1 cup frozen peas, unthawed
2 teaspoons salt
1 tablespoon chopped fresh dill, or 1½ teaspoons dried dillweed
1 teaspoon thyme, crushed
¾ teaspoon hot pepper sauce
2 teaspoons sweet paprika
½ cup olive oil, divided
2 pounds tomatoes, sliced
⅔ cup raw rice
3 tablespoons white wine vinegar
½ cup water
1½ cups shredded Monterey Jack or mild cheddar cheese

In a large bowl, toss together potatoes, eggplant, zucchini, peppers, onion, carrots, peas, salt, dillweed, thyme, pepper sauce, paprika and ¼ cup oil.

Oil a 2½-quart casserole and layer half the sliced tomatoes on the bottom. Cover with half the vegetables. Sprinkle the rice over the vegetables; layer the remaining vegetables and tomato slices.

Mix together ¼ cup oil, vinegar and water and pour over the tomatoes. Cover and bake in a preheated 325-degree oven for 2 hours. Uncover, sprinkle with the cheese and put under the broiler for 2–3 minutes, or until the cheese begins to bubble and brown.

Serves 6.

Minnesota Wild Rice with Chicken Casserole

*O*f *course there is no real substitute for the nutty flavor and crisp texture of wild rice, but it is also not a low-budget item. A combination of wild rice and brown rice is a successful and less costly alternative.*

1 tablespoon butter
1 tablespoon olive oil
½ pound small mushrooms, washed, patted dry and quartered
2½ cups chicken broth, divided
1½ cups wild rice, soaked in cold water 1 hour and drained
1 poached chicken breast, skin and fat removed and cut into ½-inch strips
½ cup sliced green onions

1 teaspoon salt
¼ teaspoon pepper
1 teaspoon thyme
½ teaspoon rosemary, crushed
½ cup light cream
2 tablespoons dry sherry
½ cup chopped parsley
1 cup herbed croutons
1 cup shredded Swiss or Jarlsberg cheese

In a large skillet, over high heat, melt the butter and oil and saute the mushrooms until they begin to brown. Stir in 1½ cups chicken broth and wild rice, or combination of wild and brown rice, and bring to a boil. Transfer to a 2-quart casserole and stir in chicken strips, green onions, salt, pepper, thyme, rosemary and cream. Bake, uncovered, in a preheated 325-degree oven 1 hour; stir after 30 minutes.

Increase the oven temperature to 375 degrees and stir in the remaining chicken broth, sherry and parsley. Sprinkle with the croutons and bake 45 minutes. Sprinkle with the shredded cheese and bake 5 minutes or until cheese melts.

The casserole can be baked up to the point of adding the additional broth, sherry and parsley. Cool, then cover and refrigerate 1 day before reheating. Add 10 minutes to the baking time.

Serves 6.

Flavorful Brown Rice and Vegetable Casserole

This casserole has so much taste and texture it will never become a bore. It can stand on its own as a main dish or serve as a side dish with a roast or grilled chops.

¾ cup brown rice, cooked according to package directions
1 tablespoon olive oil
1 tablespoon butter or margarine
1 cup chopped onion
2 garlic cloves, minced
1 tablespoon fresh dill, minced, or 1 teaspoon dried dillweed
½ teaspoon thyme, crushed
½ teaspoon marjoram, crushed
½ pound mushrooms, washed, patted dry and sliced
2 stalks broccoli, about ½ pound, top 3 inches of stems peeled and thinly sliced, florets broken into small pieces and tough lower stems discarded
¼ cup pine nuts or raw cashews, toasted
½ cup chopped parsley
1 teaspoon salt
1 teaspoon hot sesame oil, or ¼ teaspoon red or cayenne pepper
1½ cups shredded Gruyere or Jarlsberg cheese, about 6 ounces

In a large skillet, heat olive oil and butter and saute the onions until wilted. Stir in garlic, dill, thyme, marjoram, mushrooms and broccoli. Cook only until broccoli becomes tender but is still crisp. Stir in pine nuts, parsley, salt and sesame oil or pepper.

Butter a 2-quart casserole and spread with the cooked rice. Cover with the vegetable mixture and sprinkle with the cheese. Bake uncovered for 20 minutes in a preheated 350-degree oven.

The casserole can be prepared ahead up to the point of baking, but do not sprinkle with the shredded cheese. Cool, cover and refrigerate 1 day. Remove from the refrigerator 1 hour before baking. Bake, covered, in a preheated 350-degree oven for 15 minutes. Uncover, sprinkle with the shredded cheese and bake an additional 15 minutes.

Serves 6.

New Delhi Pilaf
with Broccoli and Carrots

This casserole has many of the flavors of Indian cooking—cumin, cardamom seeds and cinnamon—but it is more subtle than a curry dish.

3 tablespoons olive oil

2 teaspoons cumin seeds

4 cardamom pods, cracked open, seeds reserved and pods discarded

6 black peppercorns

2 3-inch cinnamon sticks

2 bay leaves

½ teaspoon turmeric

¾ cup brown rice

½ cup barley

2½ cups water, heated

1 teaspoon salt

2 tablespoons olive oil

2 broccoli stalks, florets broken into small pieces, 3 inches of top stem peeled and sliced ¼-inch thick, tough lower stems discarded

1 cup coarsely chopped carrots

4 garlic cloves, thinly sliced

½ teaspoon salt

½ cup coarsely chopped raw cashews, available at Middle Eastern groceries and large supermarkets, or almonds

½ cup chopped cilantro or parsley, for garnish

1 cup plain yogurt, mixed with 2 teaspoons grated lemon rind and ¼ teaspoon freshly ground black pepper

Heat the oil in a large saucepan and stir in the cumin seeds, cardamom seeds, peppercorns, cinnamon sticks, bay leaves and turmeric. Heat until cumin seeds start to pop. Stir in the rice and barley and saute about 2 minutes, stirring constantly. Slowly add water and 1 teaspoon salt and bring to a boil; cover and simmer 45 minutes, stirring once.

Heat 2 tablespoons oil in a large skillet over medium heat. Stir in broccoli and carrots and saute 3 minutes. Add garlic, salt and cashews; saute 2 minutes. Partially cover and keep warm.

Transfer the rice and barley pilaf to a 3-quart casserole and gently mix in the broccoli and carrots. Sprinkle with garnish. Serve the pilaf with a spoonful of the yogurt mixture.

Serves 6.

Basmati Rice with Zucchini and Sweet Red Peppers

Basmati rice is an aromatic rice from India or Pakistan and is available in most supermarkets. Texmati rice grown in the U.S. has the same fragrance and fluffy texture.

1 cup Basmati or Texmati rice, cooked as package directs
2 tablespoons olive oil
1 cup chopped onion
3 garlic cloves, minced
4 cups cubed zucchini, cut in ½-inch cubes
1 large red pepper, cut in ½-inch squares
2 tablespoons torn fresh basil leaves, or 1½ teaspoons dried basil, crushed
2 teaspoons fresh marjoram leaves, or ½ teaspoon dried marjoram, crushed
½ teaspoon salt, or more to taste
¼ teaspoon freshly ground black pepper
1 large egg
1½ cups low-fat cottage cheese
¾ cup chopped parsley

Cook the rice the previous day, cover and refrigerate, or cook early the day of serving and set aside.

In a large skillet, heat the oil and saute the onions until wilted. Stir in the garlic, zucchini and sweet pepper. Cook about 5 minutes; do not brown. Remove from the heat and stir in the basil, marjoram, salt and pepper.

In a large bowl, beat the egg and mix in the cottage cheese. Stir in the reserved rice and zucchini mixture. Taste for salt and adjust if necessary. Stir in the parsley just before baking.

Butter a 2-quart casserole and pour in the rice and zucchini mixture. Bake in a preheated 325-degree oven for 45 minutes.

Serves 6.

Risi e Bisi

*H*ere *is a variation of an Italian favorite found in village trattorias. Serve with a plate of grilled sweet peppers and eggplant, drizzled with extra-virgin olive oil and balsamic vinegar and garnished with fresh basil leaves.*

2 tablespoons olive oil
1 tablespoon butter
1 medium onion, chopped
1 cup shredded salty ham or prosciutto
1½ cups Arborio rice or other short-grain rice (Arborio rice can be found in Italian groceries or large supermarkets)
3½ cups chicken broth, heated
1½ cups frozen tiny peas, thawed
2 tablespoons butter
¼ cup freshly grated Parmesan cheese
Freshly ground black pepper
¼ cup chopped parsley, preferably flat-leaf

Heat the butter and olive oil in a large saucepan and saute the onion and ham until the onion is golden. Stir in 1 cup chicken broth and the rice and cook 5 minutes. Add the remaining broth and simmer, uncovered, 20 minutes, stirring occasionally. Add the peas and continue cooking until all the broth has been absorbed.

Spoon into an attractive casserole, cover and keep warm in a preheated 250-degree oven for up to 1 hour before serving. Fluff rice with a fork and stir in 2 tablespoons butter, Parmesan cheese, freshly ground pepper and chopped parsley.

Serves 6.

Grits and Cheese Bake

*G*rits are delicious and, like rice and pasta, a terrific foil for other flavors. To create a few more converts to this Southern delight, serve this grits and cheese casserole from our **Enjoy!** cookbook.

4 cups water
1 teaspoon salt
1 cup quick-cooking (not instant) grits
2 tablespoons butter
2 cups shredded sharp cheddar cheese
2 cloves garlic, minced
2 eggs, well beaten
¼ cup chopped pimento

Bring water to a boil, add salt and stir in grits in a slow, steady stream. Reduce heat to low and cook 5 minutes, stirring occasionally. Add butter, cheese and garlic. Stir until cheese is almost melted. Remove from heat. Add small amount of grits to beaten eggs; stir eggs into remaining grits. Add chopped pimento. Pour mixture into a buttered 2-quart casserole. Bake in a preheated 350-degree oven, uncovered, 35–40 minutes. Let casserole set for 10 minutes before serving.

Serves 6.

Surprise Bulgur Pilaf with Fresh Basil

*T*he surprise is the unusual combination of noodles and chickpeas that creates this unique pilaf. It is also great with bits of leftover roast lamb, beef or chicken added.

1 tablespoon olive oil
1 tablespoon butter
½ cup broken, uncooked fine egg noodles
1 cup bulgur
3 cups chicken broth, or half broth and half water
1 cup canned chickpeas, drained
1 teaspoon salt
¼ teaspoon pepper
⅓ cup torn fresh basil, or ⅓ cup sliced celery and 1 tablespoon dried basil, crushed
¼ cup coarsely chopped pecans or walnuts

Heat oil and butter in a large saucepan over medium heat. Add noodles and saute, stirring constantly until noodles are golden. Stir in bulgur and continue to saute 2 minutes. Slowly add the chicken broth and chickpeas, salt, pepper, fresh basil (or celery and dried basil) and nuts. Bring to a boil, cover and reduce heat; simmer 25 minutes.

Transfer to an attractive 2-quart casserole, fluff with a fork and serve. Or cover and keep warm in a preheated 250-degree oven for up to 1 hour before serving.

In addition to leftover meat or poultry, you could also add sauteed sliced mushrooms and onions.

Leftovers keep well and are easily reheated on top of the stove, covered, or in the oven, also covered and at a low temperature.

Serves 6.

Bulgur Casserole with Cured Black Olives

*B*ulgur *is a coarsely milled wheat grain that we like as an alternative to potatoes or rice. This casserole has an unusual combination of ingredients for a taste treat.*

3 tablespoons olive oil
1½ cups chopped onions
¼ pound mushrooms, washed, patted dry and quartered
3 garlic cloves, minced
1 cup bulgur
1 28-ounce can Italian plum tomatoes, not drained, chopped
1 cup cured black olives, pitted and halved
½ cup dry sherry
⅓ cup chopped parsley
1 teaspoon thyme, crushed
1 teaspoon oregano, crushed
½ teaspoon salt, or more to taste
¼ teaspoon red pepper flakes
2 cups shredded sharp cheddar cheese
1½ cups coarse, crumb-style stuffing mix

In a large skillet, heat oil and saute onions and mushrooms until onions are golden and mushrooms start to brown. Stir in minced garlic and saute 2 minutes more. Stir in bulgur, tomatoes, olives, sherry, parsley, thyme, oregano, salt and pepper flakes.

Transfer to an ovenproof 2½-quart casserole and bake, covered, in a preheated 375-degree oven for 25 minutes. Remove the cover, fluff with a fork, sprinkle with the shredded cheese and top with the stuffing mix. Bake an additional 15 minutes, uncovered.

Serves 6.

Middle Eastern Bulgur Pilaf

T his pilaf has a slightly sweet overtone that makes it a fine accompaniment for yogurt-and-spice-marinated lamb shish kebab.

2 tablespoons olive oil or butter
1 cup chopped onions
1¼ cups bulgur
2¼ cups chicken broth
1 tablespoon grated orange rind
1 teaspoon grated lemon rind
½ cup chopped dates
¼ cup golden raisins
¼ cup freshly squeezed orange juice
½ teaspoon salt, or more to taste
⅓ cup pine nuts or slivered almonds, toasted
⅓ cup sliced green onions
¼ cup chopped cilantro or parsley

In a large saucepan, heat the oil or butter and saute the onions until golden. Stir in the bulgur and saute for 2 minutes, stirring constantly so that it doesn't stick and burn.

Add the chicken broth, orange and lemon rind, dates, raisins, orange juice and salt. Bring to a boil, cover, reduce heat and simmer 20 minutes or until the broth has been absorbed. Stir once during the cooking time.

Transfer the pilaf to a 2-quart casserole, fluff with a fork and stir in the pine nuts, green onions and cilantro or parsley.

The casserole can be covered and kept warm in a preheated 250-degree oven for 1 hour before serving. The pilaf is also good served at room temperature or lightly chilled.

Serves 6.

Millet with Mixed Vegetables

Millet is a grain with a slightly sweet flavor and a soft consistency after cooking. It has become a favorite in the United States in recent years because of its nutritional value . . . but we just like it for the way it tastes. Millet is available in natural food stores and large supermarkets.

Millet Preparation
2 tablespoons butter
1 tablespoon olive oil
2 cups millet
8 cups boiling water
2 teaspoons salt

Heat the butter and oil in a large saucepan and saute the millet until golden. Slowly stir in the hot water and salt and bring to a boil. Reduce the heat and simmer, uncovered, 30 to 40 minutes until soft. Stir once or twice during cooking. Remove from the heat, cover and keep warm while preparing the vegetables.

Casserole Preparation
½ pound broccoli, rinsed and tough
  stems discarded
¼ pound Brussels sprouts, rinsed and
  halved
2 tablespoons olive oil
1 tablespoon butter
½ pound small mushrooms, washed,
  patted dry and halved
½ pound baby carrots, trimmed, or ½
  pound large carrots, peeled and sliced
5 garlic cloves, minced
1 cup dry white wine
¼ cup white wine vinegar

2 teaspoons basil, crushed
1 teaspoon thyme, crushed
½ teaspoon oregano, crushed
2 bay leaves
1 teaspoon salt
¼ teaspoon pepper
4 small onions, peeled and quartered
2 cups water
3 tablespoons tomato paste
1 large red pepper, seeded and cut into
  1-inch squares
4 tablespoons butter
½ cup chopped parsley mixed with 2
  teaspoons grated lemon rind

In a large saucepan, bring to a boil enough salted water to cook the broccoli. Peel 3-inch pieces of the broccoli stems and slice ¼ inch thick. Break florets into small pieces. Drop into the boiling water and cook 2 minutes. Remove with a slotted spoon. Add the Brussels sprouts to the boiling water and cook 4 minutes. Remove with a slotted spoon and keep warm with the broccoli.

In a large skillet, heat the olive oil and butter over high heat and quickly saute the mushrooms and carrots for 2 minutes. Add the garlic and saute 30 seconds.

Remove the pan from the heat and stir in the white wine, vinegar, basil, thyme, oregano, bay leaves, salt and pepper. Return to high heat and cook 3 minutes. Add the quartered onions, water and tomato paste, bring to a boil and then simmer for 5 minutes. Add the red pepper squares and the reserved broccoli and Brussels sprouts. Cook for 3 minutes and remove to a bowl with a slotted spoon. Cover the vegetables to keep them warm.

Boil the liquid in the pan for 5 minutes, then add the butter one tablespoon at a time until it is incorporated and the sauce begins to thicken slightly. Taste for seasoning and remove the bay leaves.

Transfer the cooked millet to a buttered 3-quart casserole. Spoon the reserved vegetables over the millet and pour the sauce over the vegetables. Sprinkle with chopped parsley and lemon rind mixture and serve immediately.

The casserole can be partially covered and kept warm in a 250-degree oven for 1 hour before serving.

Serves 6.

Barley and Vegetable Medley

This is a hearty casserole that seems to warm you just by reading the ingredients. A tossed salad with apple slivers and a citrus dressing would balance your menu.

1½ pounds eggplant, peeled and cut into 1-inch cubes
Salt, about 1 teaspoon, divided
5 tablespoons olive oil, divided
¼ teaspoon pepper, divided
¾ cup chopped parsley, divided
2 medium zucchini, scrubbed and cut into ½-inch slices
1 cup sliced carrots
½ cup sliced celery
1½ cups chopped onion

3 garlic cloves, minced
½ cup barley
1 16-ounce can stewed tomatoes
1 cup beef broth
1 teaspoon oregano, crushed
1 teaspoon basil, crushed
1 teaspoon salt
½ teaspoon pepper
2 cups shredded Monterey Jack cheese, divided

Spread the eggplant cubes onto a sheet of paper towel and sprinkle with salt. Let the eggplant "weep" for 30 minutes. Pat dry with paper towels. Heat 3 tablespoons oil in a large skillet and saute the eggplant over moderate heat about 3 minutes. With a slotted spoon transfer the eggplant to a 2½-quart casserole. Sprinkle with pepper and ¼ cup parsley.

Saute the zucchini, carrots and celery for 3 minutes. Transfer to the casserole and lightly sprinkle with salt, pepper and ¼ cup parsley.

Heat the remaining 2 tablespoons oil in the skillet and saute the onions until golden and translucent. Add the garlic and barley and cook 1 minute. Stir in the stewed tomatoes, beef broth, oregano, basil, salt and pepper. Transfer to the casserole. Gently mix in 1 cup of cheese into the vegetables and barley. Sprinkle with remaining parsley.

Bake the casserole, covered, in a preheated 350-degree oven for 45 minutes. Uncover, sprinkle with the remaining cheese and bake, uncovered, 10 minutes.

Serves 6.

Kasha and Mushroom Casserole

*K*asha—*buckwheat groats—team up with sauteed mushrooms for a delectable side dish. The nutty flavor and texture of the kasha is a real taste treat for those who haven't tried it before.*

½ pound mushrooms, sliced
1 medium onion, diced
1 stick butter, divided
2 cups coarse buckwheat groats
2 eggs, lightly beaten
4–5 cups chicken broth
½ teaspoon salt, or more to taste
¼ teaspoon freshly ground pepper, or more to taste

In a large skillet with a cover, brown mushrooms and onion in ½ stick butter. Remove mushrooms and onion from pan and place in a covered 2-quart casserole.

Add to skillet the remaining ½ stick butter, kasha and eggs. Cook while stirring over medium heat about 10 minutes or until kasha is dry. Add 4 cups of the broth and the salt and pepper. Bring mixture to a boil, cover and reduce heat to a simmer. Cook about 20 minutes, stirring frequently.

Add kasha to casserole with mushrooms and onion, stir, cover and bake in a preheated 375-degree oven about 20 minutes; add more broth if mixture becomes too dry. When kasha is cooked, fluff with a fork and serve from the casserole.

Serves 6.

Mixed Grain Casserole

This dish can easily stand on its own, but it is also a wonderful foil for a roast leg of lamb, a sage-and-lemon-stuffed roast chicken or a broiled bourbon-and-soy-marinated flank steak.

3 tablespoons olive oil
1½ cups chopped onion
4 green onions, sliced
4 garlic cloves, minced
3 cups beef broth
½ cup barley
2 cups chicken broth
½ cup wild rice, or brown rice

1 teaspoon oregano, crushed
1 teaspoon basil, crushed
½ teaspoon fennel seeds
½ cup bulgur
¼ cup lentils
1 teaspoon salt
¼ teaspoon pepper
½ cup chopped parsley

Heat the oil in a large saucepan and saute the chopped onions until golden. Stir in the green onions and garlic and cook 2 minutes. Add the beef broth and barley and bring to a boil; cover, reduce heat and simmer 30 minutes.

Stir in the chicken broth, wild rice, oregano, basil and fennel seeds. Bring to a boil, cover and simmer 25 minutes. Stir in bulgur, lentils, salt and pepper. Cover and continue to cook 25 minutes. Transfer to a 2½-quart casserole and keep warm in a preheated 250-degree oven for 1 hour before serving time. Stir in chopped parsley before serving. This is a moist casserole, so all the broth will not be absorbed.

Serves 6.

Mushrooms Au Gratin

This recipe first appeared in our **Enjoy!** *cookbook. Two people have told us it has become a favorite company casserole. We repeat it here in the hope that at least two more cooks will join the bandwagon!*

1½ pounds mushrooms, thickly sliced
1 cup grated cheddar cheese
1 cup black olives, pitted and sliced
2 tablespoons flour
1 teaspoon salt
¼ teaspoon pepper
½ cup light cream
2 tablespoons butter
1 cup fresh bread crumbs

In a 1½-quart buttered casserole, layer half of the mushrooms, cheese and olives. Repeat with remaining mushrooms, cheese and olives.

Mix together flour, salt, pepper and light cream. Pour over casserole.

In a small saucepan, melt butter, add bread crumbs and toss. Sprinkle over casserole. Bake in a preheated 350-degree oven for 30 minutes until bubbly and lightly browned.

Serves 6 as a side dish.

Vegetable Strudel

This caserole comes in its own "container"—phyllo pastry—for a beautiful presentation. The peas, onion and potato filling is lightly curried; we suggest you serve mango or other chutney and yogurt mixed with fresh mint on the side.

2 pounds boiling potatoes, peeled and cut into a ½-inch dice
2 cloves garlic, finely minced
1 16-ounce bag tiny frozen onions, thawed and drained
2 10-ounce boxes frozen petit pois or regular peas, thawed
4 tablespoons butter
4 tablespoons flour
1 tablespoon curry powder
½ teaspoon ground cumin
1½ cups milk
¼ cup parsley, finely minced
4–5 fresh mint leaves, finely minced, optional (do not use dried mint)
1 teaspoon garam masala (available in Indian and Middle Eastern markets)
½ teaspoon salt, or more to taste
¼ teaspoon freshly ground pepper, or more to taste
28 sheets frozen phyllo dough, thawed and covered with a damp cloth to prevent drying
1½ sticks butter, melted

Boil diced potatoes in lightly salted water until just tender, about 10 minutes; do not overcook. Drain and place in large bowl.

In a large frying pan, cook the garlic, onions and peas in the butter over low heat about 10 minutes, until very hot and peas are done. Remove vegetables with a slotted spoon and add to bowl with potatoes. Sprinkle the flour, salt, pepper, curry powder and cumin over the remaining butter (add another tablespoon of butter if necessary) and cook over medium heat about 2 minutes, stirring constantly; do not brown flour. Slowly add the milk and cook, stirring, until mixture thickens. Stir in the parsley, optional mint leaves and garam masala.

Blend sauce with the vegetable mixture. Taste for seasonings and correct as necessary. Set aside to cool.

Preheat oven to 375 degrees. Grease a large cookie sheet and set aside. On a work surface, lay out one sheet of phyllo and brush with the melted butter; repeat with 13 more sheets of phyllo, stacking sheets on top of each other. Spread half the vegetable mixture on the phyllo sheets, leaving a 3-inch margin all the way around. Fold in the short ends of the phyllo, then fold over the long sides, overlapping in the center; brush with butter to seal. Very carefully transfer to the greased cookie sheet, placing the seamed side down. Repeat steps with remaining phyllo and vegetables. Brush tops of strudel loaves with butter. Bake about 25–35 minutes until golden brown. Serve immediately.

Makes two strudel loaves; serves 6 generously.

Baked Corn and Cheese

*T*his tasty corn custard is a good accompaniment to a baked ham or roast chicken. If it's baked in a large ring mold, when unmolded the center can be filled with lima beans or other green vegetable of your choice.

2 boxes frozen corn kernels
2 tablespoons butter
8 ounces Monterey Jack cheese, grated
4 eggs
1½ cups milk
1 teaspoon Worcestershire sauce
3–4 dashes hot pepper sauce
½ teaspoon salt, or more to taste
¼ teaspoon freshly ground pepper, or more to taste

Cook the frozen corn in lightly salted water until just done, about 2–3 minutes. Drain well and season generously with butter, salt and pepper. Let cool.

Beat the eggs until light, then add the milk and the two sauces. Stir in the corn and the cheese. Taste for seasonings and adjust as necessary.

Preheat oven to 350 degrees. Pour corn mixture into a well-buttered 2½ or 3-quart glass baking dish or ring mold; set container in another pan containing hot (but not boiling) water. Bake about 40 minutes or until a knife inserted near the edge comes out clean. Let stand about 10 minutes before serving.

Serves 6.

Ratatouille

This classic vegetable casserole can be served hot or cold. To vary the dish, add one 16-ounce can of drained chickpeas. You can also bake the casserole in a 375-degree oven, stirring occasionally.

1 firm, unblemished eggplant, about 1 pound, washed and cut into one-inch cubes
3 small zucchini, washed, trimmed and sliced
1 large onion, peeled and sliced
2 large green peppers, seeded and cut into long strips
2 medium tomatoes, cut into wedges
3 cloves garlic, minced
1 bay leaf
1 teaspoon basil, crushed
½ teaspoon thyme
1 teaspoon salt
¼ teaspoon freshly ground pepper, or more to taste
4 tablespoons olive oil
¼ cup chopped parsley

In a 3-quart flameproof casserole, heat the olive oil and saute the eggplant in batches until lightly browned. Add remaining ingredients, except parsley, to eggplant and oil. Bring to a boil, reduce heat and simmer vegetables, uncovered, for 30 to 40 minutes, until liquid thickens and vegetables are cooked but still distinguishable. Stir in parsley after cooking.

Cool, cover and refrigerate at least 24 hours to allow flavors to blend. Before serving, taste for seasoning and adjust to taste; remove the bay leaf. Ratatouille can be served cold or reheated.

Serves 6.

Spinach and Artichoke Pie

A phyllo-topped vegetable and cheese custard that uses frozen artichoke bottoms and spinach for convenience. Squares of the pie make an interesting first course for a meal with Greek overtones, such as a roast leg of lamb with garlic and rosemary. Phyllo pastry sheets are available frozen in most supermarkets.

2 boxes frozen artichoke bottoms, thawed and drained
3 tablespoons olive oil
2 medium onions, thinly sliced
2 boxes frozen chopped spinach, thawed and squeezed dry
½ cup pine nuts
2 tablespoons butter
4 eggs
1 teaspoon dillweed
2 ounces feta cheese, crumbled
16-ounce carton ricotta cheese
1 cup grated Parmesan cheese
¼ teaspoon grated nutmeg
½ teaspoon salt, or more to taste
¼ teaspoon freshly ground pepper, or more to taste
14 sheets phyllo dough, covered with a damp cloth
1 stick butter or margarine, melted

Slice thawed artichoke bottoms into thin slices crosswise. Heat the olive oil in a large frying pan and saute the artichokes and onions until lightly crisp. Season lightly with salt and pepper and let cool. Add the squeezed-dry spinach, mix and set aside.

Saute the pine nuts in the butter until lightly brown. Add nuts and butter to the vegetable mixture.

In a mixing bowl, beat the eggs until light, then add the ricotta, feta and Parmesan cheeses and nutmeg and blend well. Stir the egg and cheese mixture into the vegetables. Add salt and pepper to taste.

Butter a 9 x 13-inch glass baking dish. Working quickly and keeping unused phyllo sheets covered with a damp cloth so they do not dry out, place a sheet of the phyllo in the baking dish and brush with the melted butter; repeat with 6 more of the phyllo sheets. Spoon the vegetable and cheese mixture into the dish and smooth out top. Top with the remaining sheets of phyllo, again buttering each sheet. Tuck any overlapping edges into dish.

Bake in a preheated 425-degree oven for 25 minutes. Remove from oven and let rest for at least 20 minutes. Cut into squares and serve warm or at room temperature.

Serves 6 generously.

Green Greens and Cheese Casserole

Here is a healthful entree for vegetarians; it is also a great side dish to serve with a simply prepared fish, poultry or meat entree.

1 pound fresh spinach, well rinsed, tough stems removed and leaves roughly sliced
1 bunch large leeks, split lengthwise, well washed and all but three inches of green leaves discarded; leeks then sliced in ½-inch pieces
1 cup chopped Swiss chard
2 large eggs
1 tablespoon cornmeal
2 teaspoons sesame seeds, toasted
2 teaspoons grated lemon rind
1 teaspoon marjoram, crushed
½ teaspoon thyme
1 teaspoon salt
½ teaspoon freshly ground pepper
1½ cups shredded Gruyere or Fontina cheese, about 6 ounces
3 tablespoons butter

In a large bowl, combine the spinach, leeks and Swiss chard. In a small bowl, beat the eggs and stir in the cornmeal, sesame seeds, lemon rind, marjoram, thyme, salt and pepper. Mix into the chopped greens and stir in the shredded cheese.

Transfer the mixture to a buttered 3-quart casserole, dot the top with butter and bake, uncovered, in a preheated 350-degree oven for 30 minutes.

Serves 6.

Amalfi Coast Eggplant Casserole

This is modeled on the dish we sampled on the terrace overlooking the shifting shades of blue of the sparkling Italian Gulf of Salerno.

4 tablespoons olive oil
1½ teaspoons cumin seeds
½ teaspoon fennel seeds
2 bay leaves
½easpoon red pepper flakes
2 teaspoons dry mustard
8 garlic cloves, sliced
1 teaspoon salt
1½ pounds eggplant, ends trimmed, sliced one inch thick and cubed into one-inch pieces
1 cup thinly sliced onion
1 16-ounce can chickpeas, partially drained
3 tablespoons tomato paste
2 large tomatoes, halved and seeds squeezed out, sliced ½-inch thick
⅓ cup torn basil leaves or chopped parsley
⅓ cup freshly shredded Fontina cheese

Heat the oil over high heat in a large skillet. Add the cumin seeds, fennel seeds and bay leaves, and saute just until the cumin seeds begin to pop and brown; remove from the heat. Stir in the red pepper flakes, dry mustard, garlic, salt, eggplant and onions.

Return to a medium heat and cook until the eggplant and onions begin to brown and become soft. Transfer to a 2-quart casserole.

Stir in the chickpeas and tomato paste and lay the tomato slices on top. Sprinkle with the basil leaves or parsley. Cover the casserole and bake in a preheated 375-degree oven for 20 minutes. Sprinkle with cheese and bake, uncovered, 5 minutes.

Serves 6.

Nuevas Chilequilas

*Southwestern cooking is all the rage now. This untraditional casserole can
be made even heartier—and even less traditional—by adding layers of
canned black beans, drained, between the cheese and tortillas. For an even
easier dish, use tortilla chips in place of the fried corn tortillas.*

1 pound Monterey Jack cheese, shredded
12 corn tortillas, quartered
⅓ cup corn oil
1 large onion, diced
3 canned jalapeno peppers, drained and chopped (or 1 fresh hot pepper,
    seeded and chopped)
1 16-ounce can cooking tomatoes, with their juice
1 teaspoon salt
1 teaspoon cumin
1 small can sliced black olives, drained

In a large frying pan, fry the tortilla wedges in the oil until crisp. Remove
and drain on paper towels. Remove all but 3 tablespoons oil from pan, add
onion and hot peppers and cook until onion is translucent. Carefully add
the tomatoes, salt and cumin and simmer, uncovered, about 25 minutes
or until somewhat thickened; chop tomatoes into small pieces as they
cook.

Preheat oven to 350 degrees. Set aside 1 cup of the shredded cheese. In a
2-quart baking dish, layer the tortillas and the remaining cheese, ending
with tortillas. Pour the tomato sauce over the tortillas and top with the
remaining cheese and the olive slices. Bake about 25 minutes until hot
and bubbly.

Serves 6.

West Virginia Bean Bake

This is a simple and delicious bean casserole, just right for picnics in the summer and accompanying an assortment of sausages in the winter. It has become a staple at our annual summer picnic in the beautiful hills of West Virginia—and now is a favorite at home in Washington, D.C. as well.

4 slices bacon, fried crisp and crumbled (or use 4 tablespoons bacon bits)
1 chopped onion
1 16-ounce can vegetarian baked beans (not drained)
1 16-ounce can black beans, drained
1 16-ounce can Great Northern or other white beans, drained
4 ounces sharp cheddar cheese, cut into ¼-inch cubes
½ cup brown sugar
2 teaspoons Worcestershire or soy sauce
¼ cup catsup
1 tablespoon Dijon-style mustard
¼ cup grated Parmesan cheese

Mix all ingredients except Parmesan cheese in large bowl, then spread in a shallow 2-quart casserole or baking dish. Sprinkle top with Parmesan. Bake approximately ½ hour in a preheated 350-degree oven until bubbly and cheese has browned lightly. Serve hot or at room temperature.

Serves six generously.

Easy Bean Casserole

This tasty, low-fat bean dish was developed on the spur of the moment one evening to help "take the curse off" the luscious if high-fat bratwurst that accompanied it. It worked: we tucked into second and third helpings of both. And the recipe couldn't be simpler.

3 cans Great Northern or other white beans, rinsed and drained
2 tablespoons olive oil
1 large onion, diced
2 cloves garlic, minced
5 stalks celery, diced
1 red or green pepper, diced
1 16-ounce can tomatoes, chopped
1 10-ounce can chicken broth
1 bay leaf
½ teaspoon thyme
½ teaspoon salt, or more to taste
¼ teaspoon freshly ground pepper, or more to taste

In a flameproof 2-quart casserole or Dutch oven, saute onion and garlic in olive oil until lightly brown, then add celery and pepper and cook slowly until limp. Add beans, tomatoes, chicken broth, and seasonings. Bring mixture to a boil, then bake, uncovered, in a 350-degree oven for 30 minutes. Remove bay leaf before serving.

Serves 6.

Bayou Red Beans and Rice

*T*here *are many variations of this recipe, some with tomatoes, some with spicy sausages. You can use our version for a base and add ingredients to suit your individual taste.*

½ pound thick sliced bacon, cut into
    1-inch pieces
2 large onions, halved and sliced
1 cup long-grain rice
3 garlic cloves, minced
1 teaspoon chili powder
½ teaspoon red pepper flakes
1 10½-ounce can beef broth

1¼ cups water
1 bay leaf
1 teaspoon thyme
1 teaspoon salt
1 cup diced green pepper
2 16-ounce cans red kidney beans,
    drained and rinsed

In a large skillet, cook the bacon over medium heat until fat is rendered and bacon is browned but not crisp. Remove bacon with a slotted spoon and discard all but 2 tablespoons of fat.

Add onion to the skillet and cook until golden. Stir in the rice, garlic, chili powder and pepper flakes and cook 1 minute. Remove from the heat and add beef broth, water, bay leaf, thyme and salt. Return to medium heat and bring to a boil. Cover, reduce heat and simmer 15 minutes.

Stir in the green pepper and red beans; continue to cook over a low heat until the broth is absorbed and the beans are heated through. Transfer to a 3-quart casserole, stir in the bacon and serve. Or cover the casserole and keep warm in a preheated 250-degree oven for up to 1 hour before serving.

The casserole can be prepared a day in advance, but do not add bacon until reheating. Stir in ½ cup additional broth and reheat, covered, over low heat on top of the stove or in a preheated 300-degree oven.

Serves 6.

Beans and Vegetables with Sweet Red Pepper Sauce

*Y*ou might like to serve this unusual dish with roast chicken that has been rubbed with olive oil and highly seasoned with minced garlic, ground cumin, coriander, thyme, freshly ground pepper and coarse salt.

½ cup dried navy or pea beans
½ cup barley
1 medium onion, peeled and studded with 4 whole cloves
2 bay leaves
1 teaspoon salt
3 cups water, divided
1 cup cubed potatoes, cut into one-inch cubes
1 small sweet potato, cut into one-inch cubes
1 cup sliced carrots, cut into ½-inch slices
1 cup frozen corn kernels, thawed
1 teaspoon ground coriander
1 teaspoon salt
½ teaspoon red pepper flakes
4 green onions, thinly sliced, for garnish
¼ cup chopped cilantro or parsley, for garnish

Sweet Pepper Sauce
2 tablespoons extra-virgin olive oil
2 large red peppers, seeded and chopped
1½ cups tomatoes, seeded and chopped
2 teaspoons sweet Hungarian paprika
½ teaspoon salt, or more to taste
½ teaspoon sugar

In a small saucepan, cover the beans with cold water, bring to a boil and cook, uncovered, 2 minutes. Cover and let stand 1 hour.

Drain beans and put into a 3-quart Dutch oven with barley, whole onion studded with cloves, bay leaves, 1 teaspoon salt and 2 cups water. Bring to a boil, reduce heat, cover and simmer 30 minutes.

Mix into the beans and barley the potatoes, sweet potato, carrots, corn, coriander, salt, red pepper flakes and 1 cup water. Cover and simmer over low heat for 1 hour. Remove the onion with cloves and bay leaves before serving.

While vegetables are cooking, prepare the sweet pepper sauce. Heat olive oil in a large skillet, stir in the red pepper, tomatoes, paprika, salt and sugar and cook over low heat for 30 minutes. Stir frequently. Cover and keep warm.

To serve the casserole, sprinkle with green onions and cilantro and pass the sweet pepper sauce in a sauce bowl to top the beans and vegetables.

Serves 6.

Hopping John, Vegetarian Style

In the South, Hopping John is traditionally eaten on New Year's Day to ensure good luck for the coming year. Most often it is made with bacon or a hambone and dried beans. This "new wave" version is terrific as a brunch side dish. Let your conscience dictate the amount of butter you add.

1½ cups white rice
1 large onion, diced
2 cloves garlic, minced
1 green pepper, diced
1 stalk celery, diced
2 tablespoons vegetable oil
2¼ cups vegetable broth (substitute chicken broth if desired)
1 scant teaspoon salt
½ teaspoon Tabasco-type sauce, or to taste
2 16-ounce cans black-eyed peas, drained
½ stick butter
1 cup seasoned bread crumbs

In a saucepan with a cover, saute the onion, garlic, pepper and celery in the oil until onion is translucent. Add the rice and cook, stirring, until most grains have turned white. Add the broth, salt and Tabasco, stir, cover and bring mixture to a boil. Turn down heat to a slow simmer and cook about 20 minutes until rice is tender but not mushy. Mix rice with beans and butter and place in an attractive ovenproof 3-quart casserole. Sprinkle with bread crumbs. Bake in a preheated 375-degree oven until bread crumbs are lightly browned and mixture is hot, about 25 minutes.

Serves 6.

Fish and Seafood

Tuna Casserole Compendium

*T*una—especially with noodles—is the bane and the delight of casserole lovers. Just for fun we've gathered a number of favorite variations of this icon of the American supper table.

Nina's Tuna-Noodle Casserole

College gave me my first taste of tuna and noodles. I like to think I have refined the dish since then. I love it at any rate.

12 ounces medium shells
8 ounces sharp cheddar cheese, cut into ¼-inch dice
3 cans water-packed white tuna (do not drain)
2 cans cream of celery soup
1 tablespoon dillweed
½ cup skim milk
½ teaspoon salt, or more to taste
¼ teaspoon freshly ground pepper, or more to taste
1 cup chow mein noodles

Preheat oven to 375 degrees.

Cook pasta to al dente stage, drain well and mix with diced cheese. Heat tuna (including liquid), soup, dillweed and milk to boiling; pour over noodles and cheese and toss well. Add salt and pepper to taste. Transfer to a 3-quart casserole, top with chow mein noodles and bake about 25 minutes until bubbly and lightly browned.

Serves 6.

Hilary's Favorite Tuna Casserole

*T*hat classic, crushed potato chips, tops this tasty casserole.

1 pound thin spaghetti
1 medium onion, diced
1 small green pepper, diced
3 tablespoons butter
1 can cream of mushroom soup
1 cup canned tomatoes, drained and chopped
½ cup milk
½ teaspoon thyme
2 cans water-packed tuna, undrained
½ teaspoon salt, or more to taste
¼ teaspoon freshly ground pepper, or more to taste
7-ounce package potato chips, crushed

Cook spaghetti until al dente, drain and set aside.

In a saucepan, saute onions and pepper in the butter until translucent; add soup, tomatoes, milk and thyme and heat until boiling, stirring often. Combine with spaghetti and tuna, add salt and pepper and put in a 3-quart casserole. Top with potato chips and bake at 375 degrees until bubbly.

Serves 6.

Mary Ann's Cheesy Noodles and Tuna

*C*heddar cheese soup is the variant here.

1 pound broad egg noodles
2 stalks celery, thinly sliced in half-rounds
1 medium onion, chopped
2 tablespoons butter
1 can cheddar cheese soup
½ cup milk
2 cans flaked tuna, drained
¼ cup pimento-stuffed olives, halved
¼ cup Parmesan cheese

Cook noodles until al dente. Drain and set aside.

In a medium saucepan, saute celery and onions in butter until soft. Add soup, milk and tuna. Heat, stirring often. When hot, combine sauce with noodles and olives in an open 3-quart casserole, sprinkle with Parmesan cheese and bake in preheated 375-degree oven about 25 minutes.

Serves 6.

Perfect Tuna Casserole Harman

This casserole has a zippy, cheesy sauce and a bread crumb topping.

1 pound corkscrew pasta
1 medium onion, chopped
2 tablespoons butter
1 can cream of mushroom soup
1 can cheddar cheese soup
2 teaspoons Worcestershire sauce
1 teaspoon Tabasco-type sauce, or to taste
3 cans water-packed tuna, undrained
1 cup fresh bread crumbs
3 tablespoons butter, melted

Cook pasta until al dente, drain and set aside.

In a saucepan, saute onions in butter until limp. Add soups, Worcestershire and Tabasco sauces and tuna, and heat to boiling. Combine with the pasta and transfer to an open 3-quart casserole. Spread bread crumbs on top and pour melted butter over bread crumbs. Bake in a preheated 375-degree oven until browned and bubbly, about 25 minutes.

Serves 6.

Stacey's Curried Tuna-Noodle Bake

*W*onder of wonders, no canned soup here, just a simple white sauce with the added enrichment of sour cream.

1 pound linguine
2 bunches scallions, chopped and including some green
2 teaspoons curry powder
3 tablespoons butter
3 tablespoons flour
1½ cup milk
2 cans water-packed white tuna, undrained
8-ounce container of sour cream
Salt and freshly ground pepper to taste
1 cup oyster crackers
3 tablespoons melted butter

Cook linguine until al dente, about 7 minutes. Drain and set aside.

Saute scallions and curry powder in 3 tablespoons butter until scallions are soft. Add flour and cook 2 minutes, stirring. Add milk and heat slowly, stirring often, until mixture thickens. Remove from heat and stir in tuna, sour cream and linguine. Season with salt and pepper to taste. Place in open 3-quart casserole.

In a small bowl, mix together crackers and melted butter; spread crackers around edge of casserole. Bake in 350-degree oven about 30 minutes.

Serves 6.

Dan's Tuna Fish-Potato Chip Casserole

A former bachelor's all-time favorite; now his kids chuckle over it. It is actually very classy: no noodles.

3 cans tuna fish, oil or water-packed, drained
2 10-ounce cans cream of mushroom soup
½ can milk
1 6-ounce package potato chips

In a small saucepan, mix the milk into the mushroom soup and heat to a simmer. Lightly crush ⅓ of the potato chips and spread over the bottom of a 2-quart casserole. With a fork, flake two cans of tuna on top of the chips. Create another layer with ⅓ of the chips, again lightly crushed, and the third can of tuna. Top the layers with the remaining, uncrushed potato chips. Pour the soup mixture over all. Bake, uncovered, in a preheated 350-degree oven for 45 minutes or until bubbly and slightly brown along the edges.

Serves 6.

Fantastic Fish

A biking trip in Nova Scotia led to the discovery of this sensational but easy casserole.

2 pounds fresh or frozen firm-fleshed fish (such as cod, scrod, haddock or halibut), cut into 1-inch pieces
½ pound feta cheese, broken into large pieces
Cooked rice or orzo (tiny oval pasta) to serve 6

Sauce
1 tablespoon olive oil
1 10-ounce box frozen pearl onions, thawed and patted dry
4 large garlic cloves, minced
2 14-ounce cans stewed tomatoes, with juice
½ cup dry white wine
1 teaspoon oregano, crushed
1 bay leaf
½ teaspoon red pepper flakes

Heat the oil in a medium-sized saucepan, add the onions and brown lightly over medium-high heat. Stir in garlic, tomatoes with juice, wine, oregano, bay leaf and pepper flakes and bring to a boil. Then reduce heat and simmer 10 minutes.

The sauce can be prepared up to 2 days in advance and reheated before adding the fish and baking.

If using immediately, pour the sauce into a 2½-quart casserole and place the fish on top. Cover and bake in a preheated 400-degree oven for 10 minutes. Scatter the feta cheese on top and bake, uncovered, 10 minutes. Serve the fish and sauce over the rice or orzo.

Serves 6.

Inman Square Fish and Rice Bake

T his is a budget-conscious fish casserole that is special enough for company but not too taxing for a busy schedule. Sliced fresh seasonal fruit over a scoop of berry sorbet would be a fine finale, and quick too. If you plan to serve this dish after a busy day, the rice and fish can be prepared the night before or early in the day and stored separately in the refrigerator.

2 cups cooked long-grain white rice
1½ pounds cod, scrod or haddock, poached and flaked
1½ cups grated mild cheddar or Monterey Jack cheese
2 eggs, lightly beaten
½ cup finely chopped onion
2 teaspoons curry powder
½ teaspoon thyme
1 teaspoon salt
¼ teaspoon pepper
¼ teaspoon red pepper flakes
½ cup dry bread crumbs
3 tablespoons melted butter or margarine
Chutney, for garnish

In a large bowl, gently mix together the rice, fish, cheese, eggs, onion, curry powder, thyme, salt, pepper and red pepper flakes.

Spoon mixture into a buttered 2½-quart casserole. Mix together the bread crumbs and butter and sprinkle over the fish and rice.

Bake in a preheated 350-degree oven for 45 minutes. Serve immediately with a spoonful of chutney alongside.

Serves 6.

Bluefish and Potato Casserole

*T*his easy fish-and-potato casserole is almost guaranteed to turn anyone into a lover of bluefish. It has a clean fresh flavor, thanks to the generous use of parsley. You could substitute other firm-fleshed fish filets if you like. Serve good French bread to dip in the tasty oil.

6 bluefish filets, about 6 ounces each
8 large baking potatoes, peeled and thinly sliced
1 large bunch parsley, minced
4 cloves garlic, minced
¾ cup best quality olive oil
½ teaspoon salt, or more to taste
¼ teaspoon freshly ground pepper, or more to taste

Mix together the potatoes, parsley, garlic, olive oil and salt and pepper to taste. Spread half the mixture in the bottom of a 4-quart casserole. Top with fish filets and then the rest of the potato mixture. Bake in a preheated 375-degree oven about 1 hour until potatoes are soft and top is lightly browned.

Serves 6.

Biscuit-Topped Salmon Bake

*C*anned salmon and vegetables in a tasty creamy sauce are topped with biscuit dough, either your own recipe or a prepared biscuit mix. If there is a refrigerator-case biscuit dough you are fond of, use that.

2 14¾-ounce cans red or pink salmon, drained, chunked and skin and bones removed
3 large boiling potatoes, peeled and cut in large dice
1 box frozen tiny peas
1 large onion, diced
3 tablespoons butter
3 tablespoons flour
1½ cups milk or half and half
1 tablespoon dillweed, or 3 tablespoons minced fresh dill
½ teaspoon salt, or more to taste
¼ teaspoon freshly ground pepper, or more to taste
Enough biscuit dough for 12 small biscuits

Boil potatoes about 10 minutes or until just tender, drain and set aside. Thaw peas. In a saucepan, saute onion in the butter until limp. Add the flour and cook 2 minutes, stirring. Slowly add the milk and heat, stirring often, until mixture thickens. Remove from heat and gently fold in potatoes, salmon, peas, dillweed and salt and pepper to taste.

Spread mixture in a 9 x 13-inch Pyrex-type baking dish and place biscuit dough in an attractive pattern on top. Bake in 375-degree oven about 30 minutes, until mixture is bubbly and biscuits are browned.

Serves 6.

Salmon Pie with Dill Sauce

*T*his is a versatile dish that can be served hot or at room temperature, which makes it a good buffet entree. The pie can also be frozen before baking. If possible, use fresh dill for the sauce.

1½ packages prepared piecrust mix (one package is not sufficient), or 2 ready-made frozen piecrusts to fit a 10-inch pie plate

1 14¾-ounce can salmon, drained, bones removed and flaked

¾ cup low-fat mayonnaise

1 envelope dry onion soup mix

¾ cup thinly sliced celery

¼ cup minced green pepper

2 tablespoons lemon juice

1 tablespoon fresh dill, minced, or 1 teaspoon dried dillweed

¼ teaspoon hot pepper sauce

Salt to taste

2 hard-cooked eggs, chopped

1 beaten egg mixed with 1 tablespoon cold water

Dill Sauce

2 tablespoons butter or margarine

1 cup low-fat mayonnaise

1 tablespoon lemon juice

2 teaspoons fresh dill, minced, or ½ teaspoon dried dillweed

½ teaspoon salt, or more to taste

¼ teaspoon freshly ground pepper, or more to taste

To make the sauce, melt the butter in a small saucepan; stir in the mayonnaise, lemon juice, dillweed, salt and pepper. Heat over a low flame just before serving.

Prepare piecrust for a two-crust pie. Fit one crust into a 10-inch pie plate; set aside. Cover the top crust with plastic wrap so it will not dry out.

Mix together the mayonnaise, dry onion soup mix, celery, green pepper, lemon juice, dillweed and hot sauce. Gently stir in salmon and hard-cooked eggs. Taste for salt and adjust if necessary.

Spoon the filling into the pie shell and cover with the top crust. Trim off any excess dough and crimp the edges together. Brush the top with the beaten egg mixture and cut steam slits into the top crust in a decorative pattern. Bake the pie in a preheated 375-degree oven for 40 minutes or until the crust is golden. Serve wedges of the pie topped with a spoonful of the dill sauce; pass the remaining sauce.

Serves 6.

Saucy Shrimp

This is a whiz to prepare early in the day and pop in the oven just as your guests arrive or when the family comes tumbling in from a full day of activities. You could combine a salad and vegetable course with a salad of crisp-cooked green beans, thinly sliced mushrooms and chopped eggs and tossed with an anchovy vinaigrette.

1½ pounds medium shrimp, shelled, deveined and cooked 3 minutes in simmering, salted water
1 tablespoon lemon juice
2 tablespoons olive oil
2 tablespoons butter or margarine
½ cup chopped red pepper
½ cup chopped onion
3 oil-packed, sun-dried tomatoes, julienned
1 teaspoon salt

¼ teaspoon red pepper flakes
½ teaspoon dillweed
½ teaspoon thyme
2 cups cooked long-grain rice
1 10½-ounce can tomato soup
1 cup light cream or chicken broth
½ cup dry sherry
¾ cup sliced almonds
¼ cup minced parsley, for garnish

Drain shrimp after cooking and place in a buttered 3-quart casserole. Sprinkle with the lemon juice and olive oil.

Saute the red pepper and onions in 2 tablespoons butter until soft; stir in the sun-dried tomatoes, salt, red pepper flakes, dillweed and thyme and cook 1 minute.

Gently mix into the shrimp the rice, pepper and onion mixture, tomato soup, cream or chicken broth, sherry and ½ cup almonds. Bake, uncovered, in a preheated 350-degree oven for 40 minutes. Sprinkle with the remaining almonds and bake 15 minutes longer. Before serving, top with the minced parsley.

Serves 6.

Shrimp "Souffle"

*H*ere *is another "make the night before and refrigerate" casserole. A fresh spinach salad with orange segments and a sesame oil vinaigrette dressing and a bowl of buttered sugar snap peas would be nice accompaniments.*

6 slices dense white bread
1 pound shrimp, cooked and cut into small pieces
½ cup thinly sliced celery
½ cup chopped onions
½ cup chopped green pepper
½ teaspoon salt
¼ teaspoon lemon pepper, or black pepper if not available
½ cup mayonnaise
2 cups milk
3 eggs
1 teaspoon basil, crushed
½ teaspoon seasoned salt, or plain salt if not available
¼ teaspoon lemon pepper, or black pepper if not available
2 cups grated sharp cheddar cheese
Paprika

Remove the crusts from 3 slices of bread and cube bread into 1-inch pieces; set aside. Cube the remaining bread, also into 1-inch pieces, and sprinkle in the bottom of a buttered 2-quart casserole dish.

Mix together the shrimp, celery, onions, peppers, ½ teaspoon salt, ¼ teaspoon pepper and mayonnaise. Spoon over the bread cubes. Cover with the remaining bread cubes.

Mix together the milk, eggs, basil, salt and pepper and pour over the casserole ingredients. Cover with plastic wrap and refrigerate overnight.

Remove from the refrigerator 30 minutes before baking. Bake in a preheated 325-degree oven for 15 minutes. Cover with the grated cheese and sprinkle with paprika, then return to oven and bake for 1 hour.

Serves 6.

Shrimp, Vegetables and Bow Tie Pasta

*T*his is a dish that works well whether it's served immediately after preparation or put in a holding pattern for a couple of hours. On hot summer days it tastes just as good at room temperature. We like serving icy mugs of a cold soup on those occasions.

½ pound zucchini, scrubbed, halved lengthwise and thinly sliced

½ pound crookneck squash, scrubbed, cut into 2-inch lengths and julienned into ¼-inch sticks

¼ pound sugar snap peas, or ½ box frozen peas, thawed

8 ounces bow-tie pasta, or another shape if not available, cooked al dente and drained

1½ pounds large shrimp, rinsed, shelled and tails left on

2 tablespoons olive oil

1 tablespoon butter

4 garlic cloves, minced

1 pound tomatoes, preferably garden fresh, cut into ½-inch dice

¼ cup sliced sun-dried tomatoes, oil-packed or reconstituted with warm water before slicing

¾ cup chicken broth, or for a richer sauce substitute light cream

½ teaspoon salt, or more to taste

¼ teaspoon freshly ground pepper, or more to taste

¼ cup chopped fresh basil, or 2 teaspoons dried basil, crushed

Heat 1 cup water in a medium saucepan; add salt, zucchini, crookneck squash and cook 1 minute. Add the sugar snap peas or thawed peas and cook 1 minute. Drain and set aside.

While pasta is cooking, heat oil and butter in a large skillet, add tomatoes and garlic and cook 3 minutes. Add reserved vegetables, shrimp, broth or cream, salt and pepper and cook, stirring occasionally, about 2 minutes or until shrimp turn pink and the broth is heated through.

Transfer pasta to a 2½-quart casserole, pour vegetable-shrimp sauce over and stir in basil. Serve immediately. Alternatively, cover and reheat in a preheated 275-degree oven for 30 minutes, or cool to room temperature and serve.

Serves 6.

Shrimp and Okra Pilau

*S*outh Carolina's Low Country—where shrimp, okra and rice are staples—is the inspiration for this casserole. For a true Southern meal, serve the dish with steamed collard greens or spinach and homemade biscuits.

3 tablespoons butter
1 tablespoon chili powder
1 medium onion, chopped
2 cloves garlic, minced
1 28-ounce can tomatoes, with their juice
1 cup chicken broth
½ teaspoon salt, or more to taste
¼ teaspoon freshly ground pepper, or more to taste
1½ cups raw rice
1½ pounds raw small shrimp, peeled
1 16-ounce can sliced okra, drained
8 slices bacon, crisply cooked and crumbled
¼ cup minced parsley, for garnish

In a 3-quart flameproof casserole with a lid, melt butter. Sprinkle butter with chili powder and cook, stirring, 1 minute. Add onions and garlic and cook, stirring, over low heat about 3 minutes until onion is soft. Stir in canned tomatoes, chicken broth and salt and pepper to taste; raise heat and simmer briskly 20 minutes; chop tomatoes as they cook.

Preheat oven to 375 degrees. Stir rice, shrimp and drained okra into tomato sauce and sprinkle with the bacon. Bake, covered, 25 to 30 minutes until rice is cooked. Add more chicken broth if mixture seems too dry before rice is tender. Garnish with the parsley and serve from casserole.

Serves 6.

Rice with Shellfish

Shrimp and scallops cooked in a spicy rice-and-vegetable mixture make a terrific buffet casserole. For a crowd, double the ingredients but cook the mixture in two casseroles.

3 stalks celery, sliced
1 large red pepper, diced
1 large onion, chopped
3 cloves garlic, finely minced
¼ cup olive oil
2 cups water
1½ cups long-grain rice
1 pound medium raw shrimp, peeled
1 pound bay scallops
½ cup canned tomato sauce
2 teaspoons salt
¼ teaspoon cayenne pepper
½ teaspoon freshly ground black pepper
½ teaspoon saffron threads
1 cup lightly cooked peas, for garnish if desired

In a 3-quart Dutch oven or flameproof casserole with a cover, gently cook the celery, red pepper, onion and garlic in the olive oil until soft. Add the water and bring the mixture to a boil. Add rest of ingredients except peas and bring to boil again.

The dish may be made ahead of time up to this point. Cool, cover tightly and refrigerate up to 2 days. To continue, bring to room temperature and complete as directed below, adding approximately 10 minutes to cooking time.

Cover and place in a preheated 375-degree oven. Bake about 30 minutes or until rice is done. Sprinkle with the cooked peas and cook 5 minutes more to heat peas.

Serves 6.

At-the-Beach Crab or Shrimp with Vegetables

Simple and delicious after a hard day at the beach. A tossed salad or a plate of sliced cucumbers, tomatoes and red onions and the always-popular loaf of crunchy, crusty bread will complete your menu. Don't forget dessert.

½ pound thick sliced bacon, cut into 1-inch pieces
1 28-ounce can plum tomatoes, chopped, not drained
2 cups peeled and diced boiling potatoes
1 cup chopped onions
4 cups water
¼ pound green beans,cut into 1-inch pieces
1 cup frozen corn kernels, thawed
1 cup frozen peas, thawed
½ cup raw long-grain rice
1 tablespoon Old Bay seasoning
2 teaspoons sweet Hungarian paprika
2 teaspoons dry mustard
1 pound lump crabmeat or 1 pound small shrimp, shelled
Salt to taste

In a 3-quart saucepan or Dutch oven, mix together bacon, tomatoes, potatoes, onions and water. Bring to a slow boil, cover, and simmer 20 minutes. Stir in the green beans, corn, peas, rice, Old Bay seasoning, paprika and mustard. Cover and simmer 20 minutes. Taste for salt and adjust accordingly.

If serving immediately, stir in the crabmeat or shrimp and cook an additional 5 minutes. Or prepare up to that point early in the day and reheat before adding the crabmeat or shrimp.

Serve in wide shallow soup bowls and sop up all that sauce with the crisp bread.

Serves 6.

Seafood Jambalaya

*M*ost often jambalaya is slowly simmered, but in this version we like the vegetables to retain some of their crispness. The scallops are also added toward the end of the cooking time so they aren't rubbery from overcooking.

2 tablespoons olive oil
1 cup chopped onions
1 bay leaf, crumbled
1 teaspoon paprika
1 teaspoon curry powder
½ teaspoon chili powder
½ teaspoon ground cumin
½ teaspoon hot sauce
½ teaspoon thyme
1 teaspoon salt
1 16-ounce can whole tomatoes, roughly chopped
1 cup sliced celery, including some of the leafy tops

1 cup sliced carrots
1 cup sliced okra, optional
2 large garlic cloves, minced
1 pound large shrimp, rinsed and shelled, with tails left on
2 cups water
½ cup raw long-grain rice
1 cup chopped red or green pepper
6 green onions, sliced
½ pound sea scallops, halved, or whole bay scallops
½ cup chopped parsley, for garnish

Heat oil in a 3-quart Dutch oven or soup pot over medium heat. Saute the onions with the bay leaf until the onions are soft. Stir in the paprika, curry powder, chili powder and cumin and cook 2 minutes. Remove from the heat and stir in hot sauce, thyme, salt, tomatoes, celery, carrots, okra, garlic, shrimp and water. Bring to a slow boil and simmer, uncovered, 20 minutes.

Stir in rice and simmer 15 minutes. Add peppers, green onions and scallops and simmer an additional 5 minutes. Taste for salt and hot sauce and adjust to taste. Sprinkle with parsley and serve immediately.

The jambalaya can be prepared 1 day in advance and reheated very slowly, but the character of the crisp vegetables will have been altered. Jambalaya is not a dry casserole, so you might add a small can of tomatoes, chopped, or additional water while reheating.

Serves 6.

Poultry

Chicken Divan

*H*ere *is a dish that has been a family staple for generations, probably for yours too. It is also easy enough for the kids to prepare so that Mom or Dad can have a night out of the kitchen. Just be sure all the ingredients are available, then let them go to work.*

4 boneless chicken breast halves, skin removed
Chicken broth or water, or 2 tablespoons margarine or olive oil
1 10½-ounce can cream of mushroom soup
¾ cup mayonnaise
½ teaspoon onion salt
½ teaspoon garlic salt
¼ teaspoon pepper
2 packages frozen broccoli spears, cooked as package directs
2 cups grated sharp or mild cheddar cheese
1 cup seasoned bread crumbs
¼ cup melted margarine

Simmer chicken breasts very gently in chicken broth or water for 20 minutes. Cool, then pull apart into large pieces. Or slice raw chicken into 1-inch strips and saute in hot margarine or olive oil for 5 minutes. Set aside.

Mix mushroom soup, mayonnaise, onion salt, garlic salt and pepper in a medium bowl.

Butter a 3-quart shallow baking dish and layer broccoli, chicken and sauce. Sprinkle cheese and then bread crumbs on top. Drizzle melted margarine on top and bake in a preheated 350-degree oven for 40 minutes.

Serves 6.

Savory Baked Chicken and Rice

This is so easy to prepare it is always embarrassing when the compliments begin to flow. To assuage your guilt, why not fuss with a special dessert?

4 chicken breast halves, split crosswise, skin and excess fat removed
6 chicken thighs, skin and excess fat removed
½ teaspoon salt, or more to taste
¼ teaspoon freshly ground pepper, or more to taste
Ground poultry seasoning or sage
½ pound mushrooms, sliced and browned in 1 tablespoon butter or margarine
1½ cups raw long-grain rice
1¾ cups chicken broth
1 10½-ounce can cream of mushroom soup
1 10½-ounce can cream of celery or cream of chicken soup
½ teaspoon salt
¼ teaspoon pepper
1 teaspoon marjoram, crushed
½ teaspoon basil, crushed
1 1⅜-ounce package dry onion soup mix

Wash and pat dry the chicken pieces and sprinkle with salt, pepper and poultry seasoning or sage. Let stand 30 minutes.

Butter a shallow 3-quart baking dish and spread the rice over the bottom. Pour the chicken broth over the rice and scatter the mushrooms on top. Arrange the chicken over the rice.

Combine the soups with the salt, pepper, marjoram and basil and spread over the chicken. Sprinkle the dry onion soup over all. Cover with aluminum foil. Bake in a preheated 350-degree oven for 1 hour. Remove foil and continue baking an additional 30 minutes.

Serves 6.

Chicken with Sausage and Rice

*T*his *has been a favorite with both family and friends, probably because it is so hearty and full of flavor. Instead of salad, serve a mix of crisp vegetables vinaigrette.*

4 chicken breast halves, excess fat and skin removed
6 chicken thighs, excess fat and skin removed
Olive oil
1 pound smoked Polish sausage, cut into 1-inch pieces
10 green onions, sliced in ½-inch pieces
2 medium green peppers, sliced
1 medium red pepper, sliced
4 cloves garlic, minced

4 tomatoes, seeded and coarsely chopped
6 sun-dried tomatoes, chopped, optional
2 teaspoons salt, or more to taste
2 teaspoons paprika
1½ teaspoons marjoram, crushed
½ teaspoon pepper
3 cups chicken broth, divided
1 cup dry white wine, or additional broth
1¾ cups raw long-grain rice
½ cup chopped parsley, for garnish

Heat 2 tablespoons oil in a Dutch oven or large skillet and brown the chicken on all sides. Remove and set aside. Brown the sausage slices, remove with a slotted spoon and set aside.

Heat 1 tablespoon oil in the pot or skillet and saute the green onions and peppers about 5 minutes. Add the garlic, tomatoes, salt, paprika, marjoram and pepper, stir together and cook 3 minutes. Stir in 2½ cups chicken broth and wine. Return the chicken to the pot, cover and simmer 25 minutes.

Stir in the sausage slices and the rice; cover and simmer 25 minutes. After 15 minutes, check whether more broth is needed.

Transfer to an attractive serving dish and sprinkle with the chopped parsley.

Serves 6.

Baked Chicken and Orzo

*O*rzo *is a rice-shaped pasta often used in Greek dishes. If you are worried about cholesterol, you can substitute margarine for the butter, or decrease the amount of butter. Nonetheless it is butter that gives this dish its soft and luxurious taste.*

6 chicken breast halves, skinned and cut in half again crosswise
2 tablespoons olive oil
28-ounce can plum tomatoes, chopped, with their juice
6 basil leaves, torn into small pieces, or ½ teaspoon dried basil
½ teaspoon oregano
1 stick butter
Salt and freshly ground pepper to taste
8 ounces orzo
2 cups chicken broth, heated to boiling

Brown the chicken pieces in the oil. While chicken is browning, simmer the tomatoes, butter, basil, oregano, and salt and pepper in an uncovered saucepan for about 20 minutes until somewhat thickened.

Place chicken in a 3-quart ovenproof casserole with a lid. When tomato sauce has cooked down, pour over chicken and place covered casserole in a preheated 350-degree oven and bake for 30 minutes. Add orzo and boiling broth to the casserole and mix gently. Recover and return to oven for 30 more minutes. If dish seems dry before orzo is tender, add more hot broth.

Serves 6.

Poached Chicken with Vegetables

*H*ere is a virtually fat-free casserole, but it doesn't lack in flavor. Squares of hot corn bread dotted with green chili peppers would be a good complement.

4–5 pounds chicken pieces, skin and fat removed
10–12 parsley sprigs
2 large stalks celery, with leaves, cut into 2-inch pieces
2 medium onions, peeled and quartered
2 large carrots, peeled and cut into 2-inch pieces
2 medium potatoes, peeled and quartered
1 teaspoon salt
½ teaspoon pepper
1 bay leaf
½ teaspoon thyme
½ teaspoon basil, crushed
2 cups chicken broth, fat removed
1 cup white wine

Wash chicken and sprinkle lightly with salt; set aside.

In a food processor fitted with the steel knife, chop the parsley, celery and onions. Transfer to a 3-quart Dutch oven or ovenproof casserole. Place a coarse shredder blade in the processor and shred carrots and potatoes. Add them to the casserole. If a processor is unavailable, finely chop and shred the vegetables with a knife and coarse grater.

Place the chicken pieces on top of the vegetables and sprinkle with the salt, pepper, bay leaf, thyme and basil. Pour the chicken broth and wine over and around the chicken.

Cover the casserole and bake in a preheated 325-degree oven for 1¼ to 1½ hours. Serve the chicken and vegetables with some of the broth in large soup bowls.

Serves 6.

Chicken and Parsley Dumplings

An old-fashioned favorite to cook on the top of the stove. Make the chicken mixture ahead of time and reheat to boiling before adding dumplings. A shortcut: Make dumplings from a packaged mix (such as Bisquick) and add parsley to the mixture.

5-pound stewing or roasting chicken
    (have the butcher cut it into quarters
    for easier handling)
Water to cover chicken
3 beef bouillon cubes
3 chicken bouillon cubes
1 onion, halved and stuck with 2 cloves
3 stalks celery, chopped
1 carrot, chopped
6 peppercorns
1 bay leaf
1 teaspoon dried rosemary

1 teaspoon Worcestershire sauce
1 cup cooked green peas, for garnish, if
    desired

Dumplings
3 cups unsifted all-purpose flour
½ teaspoon salt
½ cup shortening
⅔ cup water
1 cup parsley, minced fine and dried on
    paper towels

Place chicken in a large pot with a lid and cover with water. Add rest of ingredients (except peas and those for dumplings), cover and bring to a boil. Reduce heat and simmer for approximately 1½ to 2 hours until tender. Remove chicken from broth. When cool, pull or cut chicken into large bite-size pieces, discarding skin and bones. Strain broth through cheesecloth, a strainer or a coffee filter, and degrease (if you have the time, chill the stock; grease will congeal on top and is easily removed). Add chicken pieces and refrigerate until ready to cook dumplings.

To make dumplings, combine flour and salt in a bowl and cut in shortening until it resembles coarse cornmeal. Add water a tablespoon at a time, and mix well after each addition, until the mixture holds together. Add parsley and blend well. Bring chicken mixture to a boil and drop in dumpling dough by the heaping teaspoon; stir gently, cover and reduce flame. Simmer 20 minutes or until a test dumpling is cooked through. Transfer to bowl and garnish with the peas.

Serves six generously.

Baked Chicken and Vegetables

A low-fat, low-calorie dish. Serve it with good French bread to dip in the delicious sauce.

6 small chicken breast halves, skinned
8 large carrots, scraped and cut into matchsticks
8 stalks celery, cut into matchsticks
2 cloves garlic, minced
1 package dry onion soup mix
½ cup water
½ cup dry white wine
¼ cup wine vinegar
½ teaspoon dillweed
¼ teaspoon fennel seeds
2 tablespoons olive oil

In a shallow 9 x 13-inch casserole, layer carrots, celery and chicken. In a small saucepan, combine remaining ingredients except olive oil. Bring to boil, mixing well, and pour over casserole. Drizzle olive oil on chicken breasts.

Cover pan with foil and bake 1 hour in a 375-degree oven. Uncover pan, raise oven temperature to 450 degrees and bake 30 minutes more, until chicken is lightly browned.

Serves 6.

Heartland Chicken or Turkey with Stuffing

We have heard that this is a hit on the buffet tables of Milwaukee. If you don't have leftover chicken or turkey, poach chicken breasts in barely simmering salted water for 30 minutes, then proceed with the recipe.

1 14-ounce package seasoned stuffing mix
1 stick margarine, melted in 1½ cups hot water
Additional margarine for greasing baking dish
2½ to 3 cups cooked chicken or turkey, cubed or shredded
½ cup chopped onion
¾ cup light mayonnaise
½ teaspoon salt
¼ teaspoon pepper
1 10½-ounce can cream of mushroom soup
¾ cup water
1½ cups grated cheddar cheese

Lightly grease a 9 x 13-inch glass baking dish with margarine. Mix together stuffing mix, melted margarine and hot water. Spread half on the bottom of the baking dish.

Mix together chicken or turkey, chopped onion, mayonnaise, salt and pepper and spread over stuffing mix. Top with remaining stuffing mix. Dilute mushroom soup with ¾ cup water and spread over the stuffing mix. Cover with foil and refrigerate overnight or for several hours. Remove from the refrigerator 1 hour before baking in a preheated 375-degree oven for 40 minutes.

Remove foil, sprinkle with cheese and bake, uncovered, 10 minutes.

Serves 6.

San Francisco Chicken

*W*e arrived late one night, starving, at a charming cottage overlooking downtown San Francisco. The spectacular view took second place as we ate this marvelous chicken-noodle dish with a terrific California salad. California wine is a natural accompaniment.

12 small pieces chicken (all one kind if desired)
3 tablespoons olive oil
½ pound mushrooms, sliced
1 large onion, diced
2 cloves garlic, minced
1 inch piece fresh ginger, grated or diced fine
¼ cup salt-reduced soy sauce
¼ cup rice wine vinegar
½ cup white wine
½ cup chicken broth
¼ teaspoon freshly ground black pepper, or more to taste
1 pound linguine, boiled 7 minutes and drained

In a 3-quart Dutch oven, brown chicken pieces in olive oil and remove from pan. Saute mushrooms, onion, garlic and ginger in pan until mushrooms are lightly brown. Add chicken, liquids and pepper to taste. Bring to a boil, cover and simmer (or bake in a 350-degree preheated oven) for about 30 minutes or until chicken is tender. Add drained pasta, mix well and return to stove top or oven for 10 minutes until hot.

Serves 6.

Garlic Chicken

Don't be afraid of the amount of garlic in this dish. The blanching and baking make the garlic sweet and flavorful. Serve the casserole with terrific French or Italian bread to dip in the tasty sauce.

4–5 pounds chicken thighs and breast halves, skinned and breasts halved
   crosswise if large
4 tablespoons olive oil
Salt and freshly ground pepper to taste
10 whole cloves garlic, unpeeled but with ends sliced off
⅓ cup white wine vinegar
⅔ cup dry white wine (dry vermouth is fine)
16-ounce can plum tomatoes, drained and chopped
1 cup chicken broth
1 tablespoon chopped fresh rosemary, or 1 teaspoon dried
Pinch of nutmeg
1 jigger brandy
3 tablespoons butter, if desired

In a skillet, season chicken with salt and pepper to taste and brown in the oil. Place chicken in a covered 3-quart casserole.

Boil the garlic in water to cover for five minutes. Drain and, when cool, slip skins off. Scatter garlic over chicken. In an open saucepan, simmer vinegar, wine, tomatoes, broth, rosemary and nutmeg for 15 minutes. Add brandy and pour sauce over chicken. Bake, covered, in a 375-degree oven for 1 hour. Place chicken pieces in a serving bowl. Carefully pour sauce, in two batches, into a blender or food processor, add butter if desired, and blend until smooth. Pour sauce over chicken.

Serves 6.

Baked Chicken and Bulgur Wheat

*B*ulgur wheat makes an interesting change from rice and gives this dish a touch of the exotic, as do the pine nuts and hot pepper. Try this casserole with a tomato, onion and cucumber salad and seasoned pita bread halves crisped in the oven.

2 pounds boneless and skinless chicken breasts, cut in 1-inch pieces
3 tablespoons olive oil
1 cup bulgur wheat
2 teaspoons ground cumin
1 cup boiling water
½ teaspoon red pepper flakes
2 small red peppers, diced
3 cloves garlic, minced
3 medium onions, chopped
1 cup chicken broth
½ cup pine nuts
½ cup minced parsley
½ teaspoon salt, or more to taste
¼ teaspoon freshly ground pepper, or more to taste
12 fresh mint leaves, torn into small pieces

Mix cumin and bulgur wheat in a bowl, add boiling water, stir and set aside.

In a 3-quart Dutch oven, brown chicken pieces in oil; remove from pan. In remaining oil in pot, saute onion, peppers and garlic until onion is soft and lightly browned. Add broth and red pepper flakes, and simmer, uncovered, about 20 minutes until liquid is reduced by half.

Add chicken pieces, bulgur mixture (water should have been absorbed), salt, pepper, pine nuts and parsley. Mix well and bake in 350-degree oven, uncovered, for 20 minutes. (If mixture seems too dry, add a little more broth.) Fluff bulgur with a fork. Sprinkle with mint leaves and serve.

Serves 6.

Chicken, Sausage and Cabbage Casserole

*T*his is an adaptation of the Chicken and Cabbage casserole from our **Enjoy! Make-Ahead Dinner Party Menus** *cookbook, this time with sausages, boned chicken breasts and caraway seeds. A hearty winter dish, well-complemented by small boiled potatoes, dark bread and perhaps German beer.*

6 large bratwurst sausages, cut in half crosswise
6 boned chicken breast halves, skinned and sliced lengthwise
1 medium head green cabbage, cored and sliced into ¼-inch strips
2 large onions, sliced thin
3 cloves garlic, minced
½ teaspoon thyme
1 tablespoon caraway seeds
¾ cup dry white wine
¼ cup white wine vinegar
Salt and freshly ground pepper to taste

In a 5-quart flameproof casserole, slowly saute sausages until well browned; remove from pot. In sausage fat, saute chicken breasts until lightly browned; remove from pot. Discard all but three tablespoons fat and saute onions and garlic until soft. Add seasonings, wine and vinegar and simmer 5 minutes. Add cabbage, in batches if necessary as it cooks down. Tuck sausage and chicken into the cabbage mixture, bring to boil on top of stove, then bake, uncovered, in 350-degree oven about 45 minutes.

Serves 6.

Chicken Livers, Barley and Mushroom Casserole

This is a hearty dish that would be a snap to prepare after work. It's so easy that you could talk to the kids, help with homework or watch the news during preparation, or possibly do all three. Saute a pan of sliced zucchini and toss together a salad and dinner's ready.

2 cups cooked barley (cook the night before or early in the day)
1 tablespoon butter
1 tablespoon olive oil
1 pound chicken livers, trimmed and cut into quarters
1 large onion, chopped
½ pound mushrooms, cleaned and sliced
2 teaspoons curry powder
½ teaspoon poultry seasoning or thyme
½ teaspoon salt
½ cup water
1 tablespoon dry sherry, optional
¼ cup chopped parsley, for garnish

Heat the butter and oil over medium heat in a large skillet. Add the chicken livers, onions and mushrooms and saute until livers are lightly browned. Stir in the curry powder, poultry seasoning, salt, water and sherry, cover the pan and simmer 5 minutes. Transfer to a buttered 2-quart casserole and gently mix in the cooked barley. Bake, uncovered, in a preheated 325-degree oven for 20 minutes. Garnish with chopped parsley before serving.

Serves 6.

Snappy Chicken and Eggplant Casserole

*U*se the chicken parts that you prefer for this recipe. Easy and delicious, not to mention low in fat, the dish can be cooked on top of the stove or in the oven. Add a salad and rice or pasta and "dinner is served."

3 pounds chicken parts, washed, skin removed; larger pieces, such as breast halves, halved again and thighs and drumsticks separated
Salt, pepper and poultry seasoning
1 tablespoon olive oil
1 cup thinly sliced onions
3 cloves garlic, minced
1 large eggplant, peeled and cut into 1-inch cubes
1 16-ounce can whole plum tomatoes, drained and coarsely chopped
⅓ cup red wine vinegar
½ cup white wine
½ cup chicken broth, or eliminate wine and use 1 cup broth
½ teaspoon thyme
1 teaspoon basil, crushed
1 bay leaf
½ teaspoon salt
¼ teaspoon red pepper flakes

Sprinkle the chicken with salt, pepper and poultry seasoning. Heat the oil in a large skillet and brown the chicken, about 5 minutes on each side. Remove with a slotted spoon or fork to a 3-quart casserole dish or set aside on a platter if you plan to finish the dish in the skillet on top of the stove.

Add the onion, garlic and eggplant to the skillet and cook about 5 minutes. Stir in the tomatoes, vinegar, wine and broth. Bring to a boil, reduce heat and add thyme, basil, bay leaf, red pepper flakes and salt. Pour the sauce over the chicken in the casserole or return the chicken to the skillet.

Cover the casserole and bake in a preheated 350-degree oven for 40 minutes. Or you can cover the skillet and simmer 30 minutes, spooning the sauce over the chicken once while cooking.

Serves 6.

Party-Perfect Chicken and Eggplant

Another of our favorite chicken and eggplant combos, this is a great party dish because it freezes well and can be easily doubled in size. Add a platter of mixed chilled vegetables with a vinaigrette dressing, which can also be prepared in advance. If the weather is warm, you may want to serve a rice salad as a side dish in place of the more traditional rice pilaf.

4 chicken breast halves, skinned
2 tablespoons olive oil
1 tablespoon butter
1 large eggplant, peeled and sliced
   ½-inch thick
Olive oil for sauteing eggplant
1 large onion, chopped
2 garlic cloves, minced
3 tablespoons flour

½ teaspoon poultry seasoning
½ teaspoon thyme
½ teaspoon marjoram, crushed
½ teaspoon salt, or more to taste
¼ teaspoon pepper
½ cup dry white wine
½ cup chicken broth or water
½ pound mushrooms, cleaned and sliced
1 tablespoon olive oil

Heat the oil and butter in a large skillet and add the chicken; cover and slowly cook 30 minutes. Remove from the pan and cool. Remove the meat from the bones and set aside.

After the chicken has browned, stir the onions into the same skillet and saute until golden; add the garlic and cook another two minutes or more. Remove from the heat and stir in the flour, poultry seasoning, thyme, marjoram, salt and pepper. Return to a low heat and cook for 1 minute. With a whisk or wooden spoon, stir in the wine and broth or water, then cook until slightly thickened.

Heat a thin film of olive oil in another large skillet and saute eggplant on both sides until lightly browned. Set aside. Brown mushrooms in same pan; set aside.

Butter a 9 x 13-inch baking dish and place the chicken pieces on the bottom. Layer the eggplant slices on top and pour on the sauce. Sprinkle with the mushrooms and cover with foil. Bake, covered, in a preheated 325-degree oven for 45 minutes.

Serves 6.

Chicken Ratatouille Casserole

This casserole has an abundance of vegetables, so a simple green salad with croutons and raspberry-flavored vinaigrette dressing and a heaping bowl of rice flecked with lots of parsley would round out your menu.

3 tablespoons olive oil, divided
2 large onions, sliced
3 cloves garlic, minced
4 pounds of chicken pieces of your preference, trimmed of skin and excess fat
½ cup chicken broth or water
1 28-ounce can plum tomatoes, coarsely chopped, with juice
2 teaspoons salt
½ teaspoon pepper
2 tablespoons minced fresh basil, or 1 teaspoon dried basil, crushed
1 teaspoon oregano, crushed
1 pound eggplant, cut into 1½-inch pieces
1 pound zucchini, sliced into ½-inch rounds
1 large green or yellow pepper, cut into ½-inch strips

Heat 2 tablespoons oil in a 3-quart Dutch oven over medium-high heat and saute onions until golden. Stir in garlic and saute about 2 minutes. Remove with a slotted spoon and set aside.

Add remaining oil and brown the chicken, a few pieces at a time. Return chicken to the pot and add the broth, tomatoes and juice, onions, salt, pepper, basil and oregano. Bring to a boil, cover, reduce heat and simmer 40 minutes. Stir eggplant, zucchini and peppers into chicken and tomatoes and taste for seasoning. Adjust if necessary. Cover and simmer 20 minutes.

Serve directly from the Dutch oven or transfer to a large shallow bowl, with chicken pieces in the center and vegetables around the chicken.

Serves 6.

Chicken and Sausage Jambalaya

Makes 10 loaves + 6 cups 1¾ C

*L*ike other ethnic and "down-home" recipes, there are subtle variations of jambalaya recipes. You could add a half-pound of shelled shrimp during the last 5 minutes of cooking, or omit the sausage and add more shrimp. One young man uses strips of boneless chicken breast for a quicker-to-prepare version.

1 tablespoon olive oil, divided
1 pound smoked Polish sausage, sliced, or andouille sausage, if available
4 pounds chicken pieces, skin and excess fat removed (or 6 boneless breast halves)
1½ cups chopped onion
1 cup chopped green pepper
1 cup chopped celery
3 cloves garlic, minced
2 cups seeded, chopped tomatoes, or 1 14½-ounce can plum tomatoes, chopped
½ cup tomato sauce

½ lb Shrimp

1½ teaspoons oregano, crushed
1 teaspoon thyme
2 bay leaves
½ teaspoon cayenne pepper (if using andouille sausage use ¼ teaspoon cayenne pepper)
½ teaspoon black pepper
2 teaspoons paprika
½ teaspoon turmeric, optional
3 cups chicken broth
½ cup chopped parsley
½ cup chopped green onions
1½ teaspoons salt
1¾ cups raw long-grain rice

Heat 1 tablespoon oil in a 5-quart Dutch oven and saute sliced sausage until lightly browned. Remove sausage with a slotted spoon and set aside. Brown the chicken pieces in the sausage fat and set aside.

Stir the onions, green peppers, celery, garlic, tomatoes, tomato sauce, oregano, thyme, bay leaves, cayenne and black peppers, paprika and turmeric into the remaining fat and cook over low heat about 5 minutes.

Return the chicken to the casserole and add the broth. Bring to a boil, then reduce the heat and stir in the sausage, parsley, green onions, salt and rice. Cover and cook 30 minutes.

Stir the rice up from the bottom, cover and cook 15 minutes. If you are using shrimp, add after 10 minutes.

If you reheat the casserole, add additional hot broth if it seems dry.

Serves 6.

Creole Jambalaya

Another jambalaya recipe, this one using okra and peas for a somewhat different flavor and texture. Small chicken thighs, skinned, help reduce the fat content.

12 small chicken thighs, skinned
3 tablespoons olive oil
1 large onion, minced
1 green pepper, minced
1 red pepper, minced
3 cloves garlic, minced
28-ounce can plum tomatoes
1 cup chicken broth (bouillon and water is fine)
½ teaspoon thyme
¼ teaspoon sage
½ teaspoon Tabasco-type sauce (or to taste)
1 package frozen whole okra
2 cups long-grain white rice
½ teaspoon salt, or more to taste
¼ teaspoon freshly ground pepper, or more to taste
1 package frozen peas

In a flameproof 3-quart casserole, brown the chicken thighs in the oil; remove. Saute onions, peppers and garlic in oil until onion is limp. Add chicken and rest of ingredients, except peas, to pot and bring to boil, stirring well.

Cover and bake in a 350-degree oven about 45 minutes until rice is almost tender. Uncover and add peas, stirring into the mixture carefully. Recover and bake an additional 15 minutes. Taste for seasonings and adjust if necessary.

Serves 6.

Kentucky Burgoo

*O*ur version of this American classic wouldn't qualify as authentic: it doesn't contain a squirrel. Like so many old stew-type recipes, there are a multitude of variations. Add or eliminate ingredients according to your preferences and it will still be a burgoo (with the accent on the first syllable).

3 pounds chicken pieces, excess fat removed
1 to 1½ pounds beef shank, cross cut
1 medium onion, stuck with 3 whole cloves
3 cups water
1 16-ounce can whole tomatoes, undrained and chopped
1½ teaspoons salt
1 large onion, coarsely chopped
½ 10-ounce package frozen lima beans or peas, thawed
½ 10-ounce package frozen corn, thawed
½ 10-ounce package frozen okra, not thawed

1 cup chopped celery
½ cup chopped green pepper
1 teaspoon sugar
1 teaspoon salt
1 teaspoon thyme
1 bay leaf
1 tablespoon Worcestershire sauce
¼ teaspoon hot pepper sauce
½ cup cold water
2 tablespoons flour
½ cup chopped parsley, for garnish
Cooked rice to serve 6

In a 5-quart soup kettle or Dutch oven, place the chicken pieces, beef shank, onion with cloves, water, tomatoes and salt. Bring to a boil, reduce heat, cover and simmer 1½ hours. Remove the chicken and beef, cover with plastic wrap and cool. Reserve broth and discard onion.

Remove meat from the bones and return to the broth. Add chopped onions, lima beans or peas, corn, okra, celery, green pepper, sugar, salt, thyme, bay leaf, Worcestershire sauce and pepper sauce. Stir well, cover and simmer for 30 minutes.

In a small bowl, mix together the cold water and flour and stir into the stew. Cook until the mixture thickens slightly. Sprinkle the chopped parsley over the burgoo and serve in wide soup bowls on top of cooked rice.

Serves 6.

Chicken Tetrazzini

A time-honored dish, perfect for a buffet table or a potluck supper. It can be made ahead of time and frozen; thaw before baking. This also reheats successfully in a microwave, should there be any leftovers.

2 pounds boned chicken breast halves, skinned
12 ounces spaghetti or linguine, broken in half, cooked al dente and drained
1 pound mushrooms, cleaned and sliced
4 ounces slivered almonds
2 cups chicken broth
3 tablespoons instant-blending flour
6 tablespoons butter, divided
1 small jar sliced pimentos, rinsed and drained
½ teaspoon Tabasco-type sauce
1 teaspoon Worcestershire sauce
1 teaspoon salt, or more to taste
¼ teaspoon freshly ground pepper, or more to taste
1 cup half and half or heavy cream
3 tablespoons grated Romano or Parmesan cheese
Additional grated Parmesan for topping

Poach chicken breasts in gently simmering water for 12 minutes, then cool. Cut or tear into large bite-size pieces. Set aside.

In a large frying pan, saute the mushrooms and almonds in 3 tablespoons of the butter until lightly browned. Set aside.

To make the sauce, heat the remaining 3 tablespoons of butter in a saucepan, add the flour (instant-blending flour makes a lump-free sauce) and cook, stirring, for 2 minutes. Carefully add the chicken broth and simmer until thickened. Remove from heat and stir in pimento, Tabasco, Worcestershire, half and half, salt, pepper and the grated cheese. Combine set-aside ingredients with the sauce and spread in large shallow casserole. Sprinkle Parmesan on top. Bake in preheated 375-degree oven for about 20 minutes until lightly browned and bubbly.

Serves 6 generously.

Easy Chinese Chicken and Rice

*T*his tasty and easy-to-prepare dish is great when you have leftover rice on hand. Why get takeout when you can whip this up at home?

12 boneless chicken thighs, skinned
3 tablespoons vegetable oil
4 tablespoons dry sherry
2 tablespoons soy sauce
2 tablespoons chili sauce
2 tablespoons lemon juice
½ cup chicken broth (bouillon is fine)
1 bunch scallions, chopped and including green tops
4 tablespoons chopped parsley
Salt and freshly ground black pepper to taste
3 cups cooked rice

Season chicken with salt and pepper and brown in the oil in a 3-quart flameproof casserole. Mix sherry, soy sauce, chili sauce, lemon juice and chicken broth in a small bowl and add to pot. Cover pan and simmer 20 minutes until chicken is tender.

Remove chicken from pot and boil sauce down until slightly thickened, if necessary. Add rice and stir well to blend. Add salt and pepper to taste. Place chicken thighs on top, cover and cook over low heat about 10 minutes until rice is hot. Uncover and sprinkle with scallions and parsley.

Serves 6.

Szechuan Chicken, Rice and Peanut Casserole

A make-ahead Chinese chicken-and-peanuts dish that can be addictive. You could substitute cooked thin spaghetti for the rice to vary the dish. Serve with chopsticks and a simple salad of thinly shredded cabbage dressed with 2 tablespoons soy sauce, 1 teaspoon rice wine vinegar, ½ teaspoon sugar and 1 teaspoon sesame oil.

6 boneless chicken breast halves, skinned
4 tablespoons vegetable oil
3 whole dried hot red peppers or ½ teaspoon red pepper flakes
1 teaspoon Szechuan peppercorns
2 cloves garlic, minced
1 inch fresh ginger, diced
6 tablespoons soy sauce
2 tablespoons dry sherry
1 tablespoon sugar
2 tablespoons cornstarch
1 tablespoon sesame oil
½ cup chicken stock (more if needed)
4 cups cooked rice (or 16 ounces cooked thin spaghetti)
½ cup salted peanuts
1 bunch scallions, chopped

In a 3-quart flameproof casserole with a lid, brown the chicken breast halves in the vegetable oil and set aside. Saute the hot peppers, peppercorns, garlic and ginger in the oil until fragrant. Mix together the soy sauce, sherry, sugar, cornstarch, sesame oil and chicken stock; add to pan along with the chicken breasts. Simmer, covered, about 20 minutes until chicken is tender. Add rice or spaghetti and mix well.

Bake in 350-degree preheated oven, covered, for 20 minutes until hot. Sprinkle with peanuts and chopped scallions and serve.

Serves 6.

Mexicali Chicken

Here is a "do-ahead" casserole that satisfies everyone's Southwestern cravings. Serve with scoops of guacamole on a bed of shredded lettuce with salsa and sour cream on the side. A basket of crisp tortilla chips is always in order.

4 boneless chicken breast halves
1 medium onion, minced
2 cloves garlic, minced
Salt and pepper
10 7-inch corn tortillas
1 10½-ounce can cream of chicken soup
Canned chicken broth added to juice from cooking chicken to equal 1¼ cups
1 envelope dry taco mix
¼ teaspoon hot pepper sauce

2 canned whole chili peppers, cut into 1-inch pieces, or one 4-ounce can chopped chilies (drained and juice added to the soup mix)
1 11-ounce can Mexican-style corn, or plain yellow corn, drained
1 cup cooked pink kidney beans, drained and rinsed
2 cups shredded sharp Cheddar cheese
Salsa to pass for garnish

Place the chicken breasts on a sheet of aluminum foil and sprinkle with onion, garlic, salt and pepper. Wrap foil around chicken and bake in a preheated 350-degree oven for 40 minutes. Add the accumulated juices to the canned chicken broth. Cool the meat and shred into large pieces. Set aside.

Tear 5 tortillas into large pieces and place in the bottom of a 3-quart casserole, moistening with 2 tablespoons of chicken broth. In a medium bowl, mix together cream of chicken soup, remaining chicken broth, juice from canned chilies, dry taco mix and pepper sauce. Layer half the chicken, corn, kidney beans, chili peppers, cheese and remaining torn tortillas over the tortillas in the casserole and top with half the sauce. Repeat the layering, but end with the cheese over the sauce.

Bake uncovered in a 350-degree oven for 1½ hours. Allow to stand 10 minutes before serving. Pass a bowl of salsa separately.

Serves 6.

Tamale Chicken Pie

*S*outhwestern foods are definitely the rage and here is an easy-to-prepare combination of cornbread and the tongue-tingling taste of jalapeno peppers. A cool and unusual salad of thinly sliced jicama and orange wedges on a bed of shredded lettuce and with a lime vinaigrette dressing would go well with this casserole.

4 boneless and skinless chicken breast halves, cut into 1-inch strips
1 tablespoon olive oil
1 tablespoon butter or margarine
½ cup chopped onions
½ cup chopped green or red pepper
2 cloves garlic, minced
1 tablespoon pickled jalapeno peppers, chopped
2 teaspoons chili powder
1 teaspoon salt
½ teaspoon cayenne pepper
1 16-ounce can whole tomatoes, chopped and juice reserved
1 cup frozen corn kernels, thawed
4 cups chicken broth or water, or half broth and half water
1½ cups yellow cornmeal
1 teaspoon salt
1 teaspoon sugar
3 tablespoons chopped cilantro or parsley
2 cups shredded Monterey Jack cheese or mild cheddar cheese

Heat the oil and butter in a large skillet over medium-high heat and quickly saute the chicken pieces. Remove with a slotted spoon and set aside.

Add the onions, green pepper, garlic and jalapeno peppers to the skillet and cook over medium heat about 5 minutes. Add the chili powder, salt and cayenne pepper and cook 1 minute. Stir in the tomatoes and juice, corn and reserved chicken and any accumulated juices. Simmer, uncovered, 10 minutes. The sauce can be prepared up to 2 days in advance; reheat before assembling casserole.

While sauce is cooking, bring the chicken broth or water to a boil. Slowly stir in the cornmeal, salt and sugar. Reduce heat and continue cooking and stirring until the mixture has thickened, about 10 minutes. Stir in the cilantro or parsley.

Lightly butter a 9 x 13-inch baking dish. Spread half the cornmeal mixture over the bottom. Spoon the chicken and tomato sauce on top. Spread the remaining cornmeal over the chicken. Sprinkle the shredded cheese on top. Bake in a preheated 375-degree oven for 30 minutes or until golden brown.

Serves 6.

Santa Fe Chicken and Vegetables

*W*e haven't met a group of taste-testers who didn't give this casserole an excellent rating, even before they found how easy it is to put together.

6 slices bacon, halved
6 chicken thighs, skin and excess fat removed
4 chicken breast halves, skin and excess fat removed
¼ cup flour
1 teaspoon salt
½ teaspoon thyme
½ teaspoon ground cumin
¼ teaspoon pepper
1 cup milk
1 12-ounce can Mexican-style corn, drained and liquid reserved
1 4-ounce can chopped green chilies
1½ cups frozen peas
1 cup thinly sliced celery

Saute bacon in a large skillet until crisp. Remove and set aside. Brown chicken pieces in bacon drippings. Remove and set aside.

Off the heat, stir into the remaining drippings the flour, salt, thyme, cumin and pepper. Return to a low heat and cook for one minute. With a whisk, slowly stir in the milk and reserved corn liquid and cook until slightly thickened. Place the chicken back in the skillet and spoon the sauce on top; cover and simmer 30 minutes. Stir in the corn, chopped chilies, peas and celery; cover and simmer an additional 15 minutes.

Transfer to an attractive serving dish. Break bacon into large pieces and sprinkle on top.

Serves 6.

Arroz con Pollo

*T*he less complex—and less expensive—cousin of paella, arroz con pollo *(chicken with rice) forms the core of a Latin or Spanish-style meal. Start with a salad of sliced oranges, red onion rings, and black olives with a vinaigrette dressing flavored with oregano leaves; serve canned black beans and crusty bread with the casserole; and, for dessert, try a ring of flan, perhaps with fresh fruit in the center.*

12 small chicken thighs, skinned (or 6 large chicken breast halves, skinned and halved again crosswise)
3 tablespoons olive oil
1 medium onion, chopped
1 green pepper, chopped
2 cloves garlic, minced
28-ounce can plum tomatoes
1 bay leaf
1 teaspoon oregano

½ teaspoon saffron threads or 1 teaspoon turmeric
½ cup chicken stock
½ cup white wine
1½ cups long-grain white rice
1 cup tiny frozen peas, thawed
1 small jar diced pimento, drained
½ teaspoon salt, or more to taste
¼ teaspoon freshly ground pepper, or more to taste

In a 3-quart Dutch oven, salt and pepper chicken and brown well in olive oil. Remove from pan. Add onions, green pepper and garlic and saute until onion is soft. Chop tomatoes in can with a long knife and add contents of can to pan along with the seasonings, chicken stock and wine. Simmer mixture for 10 minutes, then add chicken and any accumulated juices; simmer about 15 minutes more or until chicken is tender. (Dish may be refrigerated up to 2 days or frozen at this point.)

Preheat oven to 375 degrees. Slowly bring mixture to a boil on top of stove, add the rice, cover and bake about 20 minutes; sprinkle peas and pimento pieces over top, recover pan and cook about 10 minutes longer or until rice is done. Serve from casserole.

Serves 6.

Paella

Construction of a paella requires a certain amount of advance planning and preparation. Timing is essential. But the final results will bring praise from all at your table.

4 chicken breast halves, excess fat and skin removed, cut crosswise and patted dry
1 teaspoon oregano, crushed
1½ teaspoons salt
½ teaspoon pepper
1 teaspoon paprika
2 cloves garlic, minced
4 tablespoons olive oil, divided
2 teaspoons vinegar
1 pound chorizo (hot Spanish sausage) or hot Italian sausage, sliced
¼ pound thickly sliced ham, cut into ½-inch strips
1 cup chopped onions
1 large green pepper, sliced
½ teaspoon ground cumin
1 teaspoon ground coriander
1¾ cup raw long-grain rice
1 cup stewed tomatoes
3 cups hot chicken broth or water
½ teaspoon saffron or turmeric
18 small clams, scrubbed
1 quart mussels, scrubbed and beards trimmed off
1 pound large shrimp, rinsed, shells left on
1½ pound lobster, steamed, cooled and meat removed and set aside, covered (optional)
½ 10-ounce package frozen peas, thawed
1 3-ounce jar whole pimentos, drained and sliced

In a small bowl, mix together the oregano, salt, pepper, paprika, garlic, 2 tablespoons oil and vinegar. Rub the mixture into the chicken. Heat the remaining oil over medium-high heat in a large skillet and brown the chicken on all sides. Remove and set aside. Cover to keep warm.

Add the sausage, ham, onions, peppers, cumin and coriander to the skillet and cook over low heat, about 10 minutes. Add the rice and stewed tomatoes and cook 5 minutes. Stir in the hot broth or water, saffron or turmeric and the chicken and cook, covered, over low heat for 20 minutes.

At this point, the mixture can be removed to a storage container, covered, cooled and refrigerated for 1 day. Before continuing, reheat the mixture in a skillet.

Cook the scrubbed clams and mussels in 2 inches boiling water for 10 minutes. Drain and discard any unopened shells. Set aside and keep warm.

Add the shrimp, lobster meat and thawed peas to the chicken and rice and mix gently, bringing the rice from the bottom to the top. Simmer, covered, 5 to 7 minutes or until the shrimp are pink and all the liquid is absorbed.

Transfer to a large, shallow serving bowl and place the clams and mussels around the edge. Garnish the top with the pimento strips. If possible, run the bowl under the broiler for 2 minutes.

When serving, be sure each person receives a sampling of the various ingredients.

Serves 6.

Chicken with Lentils and Spinach

If you have an Indian grocery nearby, serve this dish with a plate of pappadoms and other Indian breads, or warmed small pita breads, available in supermarkets. A cucumber and yogurt salad with fresh mint or cilantro is a cooling accompaniment.

1½ cups chopped onion
1 tablespoon olive oil
1 tablespoon finely minced fresh ginger root, or 1 teaspoon ground ginger
2 teaspoons cumin seeds or ½ teaspoon ground cumin
1 teaspoon ground coriander
¾ teaspoon ground cinnamon
3½ cups chicken broth or water
3 pounds favorite chicken parts, skin and excess fat removed
3 large carrots, scraped and cut into 2-inch pieces
½ cup raisins
1 teaspoon salt
1½ cups lentils, rinsed and picked over
1 pound spinach, washed of all sand and tough stems removed, or 1 10-ounce package frozen spinach, thawed and squeezed dry

Heat the oil in a large skillet or Dutch oven and saute the onions until golden. Stir in the ginger, cumin, cinnamon and coriander and saute briefly, until the spices become fragrant.

Stir in the broth or water, then add the chicken, carrots, raisins and salt. Cover and bring to a boil, then reduce heat and simmer 20 minutes. Stir in the lentils and simmer 30 minutes. If lentils are not quite soft (they shouldn't be mushy), simmer an additional 5 or 10 minutes. Stir in spinach and cook 5 minutes.

Spoon into an attractive casserole and serve.

Serves 6.

Exotic Chicken with Dried Fruit and Nuts

*T*his chicken dish has a Middle Eastern flair. It can be served with rice or couscous, but for a change try pita rounds, halved lengthwise, sauteed in a mixture of butter, olive oil and finely minced garlic and sprinkled lightly with salt.

8 large chicken breast halves, skinned and cut in half crosswise
1 teaspoon ground cumin
½ teaspoon ground cinnamon
1 teaspoon ground turmeric
1 teaspoon ground coriander
1 teaspoon salt
3 tablespoons olive oil
1 large onion, chopped
3 cloves garlic, minced
½-inch piece fresh ginger, minced
1½ cups chicken broth
8-ounce package mixed dried fruit, chopped
½ cup whole blanched almonds, sauteed in oil until light brown
2 tablespoons fresh coriander, chopped, for garnish if desired (or substitute parsley)

Mix together ground spices and salt and sprinkle over chicken pieces; let stand for ½ hour. Heat oil in skillet and brown the seasoned chicken. Place chicken in a 3-quart flameproof casserole with a lid. In skillet, saute onion, garlic and ginger until onion is wilted. Add chicken broth and chopped fruit and bring to boil. Pour over chicken, add almonds and simmer, covered, for 30 minutes, until fruit and chicken are tender. If desired, thicken sauce by uncovering casserole for last 15 minutes of cooking. Sprinkle with coriander or parsley.

Serves 6.

Nasi Goreng

This is an Indonesian version of chicken curry that lets everyone be creative with the condiments offered. It also makes a good choice for a buffet entree, as it doesn't require a knife and can be prepared in advance of serving.

Chicken Preparation
3 pounds chicken breasts and thighs, excess fat removed
8 peppercorns
1 small onion, stuck with 2 whole cloves
2 teaspoons salt
1 bay leaf
Water to cover chicken

Place chicken in a large saucepan and add peppercorns, the onion with cloves, salt and bay leaf. Cover with cold water and heat slowly to the boiling point. Reduce heat, cover pan and simmer 30 minutes. Remove chicken from the pan and cover lightly with plastic wrap until cool. Strain and reserve chicken broth. Remove chicken from the bones and cut into large bite-size pieces. Cover and set aside.

Casserole
1¾ cups raw long-grain rice
4 cups chicken broth (add canned broth to reserved broth), divided
¼ cup peanut or vegetable oil
1 cup chopped onions
4 cloves garlic, minced
½ teaspoon red pepper flakes
2 teaspoons ground coriander
1 teaspoon ground cumin
4 cardamom pods, seeds removed and pods discarded, or ½ teaspoon ground cardamom
½ teaspoon pepper
3 tablespoons creamy peanut butter
1 cup diced ham
Reserved chicken
½ pound medium-sized shrimp, rinsed and shelled

Condiments
Chutneys (Besides mango, look for one or two unusual mixes.)
Diced cucumbers
Shredded carrots with a bit of grated fresh ginger root
Finely shredded lettuce
Thinly sliced and crisply fried onions
Finely chopped peanuts
Soy sauce

Stir rice into 3½ cups boiling chicken broth, cover, reduce heat and simmer 20 minutes or until the broth is absorbed. Spread rice out on baking sheets to cool and dry.

Heat oil in a 5-quart skillet or Dutch oven, add chopped onions and cook 5 minutes. Stir in garlic, red pepper flakes, coriander, cumin, cardamom seeds and pepper and cook 2 minutes until the spices are fragrant. Mix in peanut butter and cooled rice and cook 2 minutes over low heat.

Gently stir in ham, chicken and shrimp and ½ cup reserved chicken broth. Cover and bake in a preheated 300-degree oven for 30 minutes. This casserole is meant to be somewhat dry.

Place condiments in separate small bowls, place bowls on a tray or Lazy Susan and let everyone select their favorites.

Serves 6.

Chicken Tagine

agines are Moroccan versions of slowly simmered, aromatic stews. Couscous, which is semolina made from durum wheat that has been steamed and dried to a granular shape, is generally served with a tagine, but rice is equally appropriate.

3 or 4 chicken breast halves, skin and fat removed and halved crosswise

6 chicken thighs, skin and fat removed

3 tablespoons olive oil, divided

2 cups coarsely chopped onions

4 cloves garlic, minced

4 cups chicken broth

3 3-inch cinnamon sticks, broken in half

2 bay leaves

2 teaspoons curry powder

2 teaspoons ground cumin

1 teaspoon ground coriander

1/4 teaspoon saffron threads, if available, or 1/2 teaspoon turmeric

1 1/2 teaspoon salt

1/2 teaspoon ground pepper

3 large carrots, peeled and cut into 1-inch pieces

2 medium zucchinis, scrubbed, halved lengthwise and sliced

2 medium potatoes, peeled and cut into 1/2-inch dice

1 large green pepper, sliced

3 ripe tomatoes, seeded and cut into slim wedges

6 pitted prunes, halved

6 dried apricots, halved

1 cup golden raisins

1/2 cup chopped cilantro or parsley, for garnish

1/2 cup toasted pine nuts, to mix with couscous or rice, optional

Heat 2 tablespoons oil in a 5-quart Dutch oven or large skillet. Brown chicken on all sides, a few pieces at a time. Remove and set aside. Add 1 tablespoon oil to the pot or skillet and stir in chopped onions; saute until golden. Add garlic and cook 1 minute more. Stir in chicken broth, cinnamon sticks, bay leaves, curry powder, cumin, coriander, saffron or turmeric, salt and pepper and bring to a boil.

Return chicken and any accumulated juices to the pot, add the carrots, zucchini and potatoes and simmer, uncovered, for 30 minutes. Stir in sliced peppers, tomatoes, prunes, apricots and raisins and simmer 15 minutes.

Serve in wide soup bowls over couscous or rice. Garnish with the chopped cilantro or parsley.

Serves 6.

Turkey and Rice with Peppers and Spinach

*H*ere *is a wonderfully flavorful and healthful combination that is quick to prepare after work or play. For menu variety, serve with a cold soup instead of a salad.*

2 tablespoons olive oil, divided
1½ pounds ground turkey (for less fat content, grind turkey breast meat or turkey cutlets in the food processor)
1½ cups raw long-grain rice
½ cup chopped parsley
1 teaspoon marjoram, crushed
1 teaspoon grated fresh ginger root, optional
1 teaspoon salt
½ cup dry white wine
3½ cups hot chicken broth or water
1 green pepper, sliced
1 red pepper, sliced
6 green onions, sliced in 1-inch pieces
2 cloves garlic, minced
3 cups fresh spinach leaves, thoroughly washed, tough stems removed and cut into ½-inch strips, or 1 10-ounce package frozen chopped spinach, thawed

In a large saucepan, heat 1 tablespoon oil over medium heat and saute the ground turkey for 3 or 4 minutes. Add the rice, parsley, marjoram, grated ginger, salt and wine and cook for 5 minutes. Stir in the broth or water, reduce the heat and simmer 20 minutes.

While the turkey and rice are cooking, heat the remaining 1 tablespoon oil in a large skillet over medium heat and saute the peppers about 5 minutes. Add the green onions, garlic and spinach and cook 3 minutes, sprinkling with salt and pepper.

Stir the vegetables into the turkey and rice and transfer to an attractive serving dish.

Serves 6.

Turkey and Brown Rice Casserole

T his casserole packed with "carbs" and lean protein is good for your mental health as well, since it's so easy to whip together. A delicious use for post-holiday leftovers too.

3 cups cooked turkey
3½ cups cooked brown rice
1 cup chopped celery
1 cup chopped green pepper
3 tablespoons butter
½ cup white wine or chicken broth
1 10½-ounce can cream of mushroom soup, undiluted
1 6-ounce can sliced mushrooms, undrained
1 4-ounce can pimento, drained and chopped
1 tablespoon crumbled sage leaves
½ teaspoon salt
¼ teaspoon thyme
Dash of pepper
1 cup herb-seasoned croutons

Combine turkey and rice in a greased 2½-quart casserole. Set aside.

Preheat oven to 350 degrees. In a large skillet, saute onion, celery and green pepper in 2 tablespoons butter, stirring frequently until tender but crisp. Stir in soup, wine or broth, mushrooms, sage, salt, thyme, pepper and pimentos. Pour contents of skillet over rice and turkey in casserole. Stir well to combine.

In same skillet, heat the remaining tablespoon of butter. Toss croutons in the melted butter and sprinkle on top of the casserole. Bake 40 to 45 minutes.

Serves 6.

Turkey Lasagna
with Mornay Sauce

*Y*ou *don't have to wait for leftover turkey to make this wonderful casserole. Sprinkle a turkey breast with salt, pepper, poultry seasoning or sage, chopped onion and minced garlic, wrap in aluminum foil and roast for the prescribed time. Use the broth collected in the foil for the recipe.*

12 lasagna noodles, cooked al dente, rinsed and drained

4 tablespoons butter or margarine

½ cup chopped onions

3 tablespoons flour

1 teaspoon salt

½ teaspoon pepper

½ teaspoon thyme

¼ teaspoon nutmeg

2 cups warm chicken broth, or leftover turkey broth

1 cup warm milk

½ cup freshly grated Parmesan cheese

½ cup freshly grated Romano cheese, or use all Parmesan cheese

⅓ cup dry sherry

8–10 slices turkey breast, depending on the size, to make 2 layers in the baking dish, or about 4 cups small pieces cooked turkey

12 ounces low-fat mozzarella cheese, sliced

1 pound mushrooms, washed and sliced

3 tablespoons freshly grated Parmesan cheese

1 16-ounce can whole cranberry sauce mixed with grated orange rind and cinnamon, for garnish

In a medium saucepan, melt butter or margarine and saute onions until limp and golden. Remove from the heat and whisk in flour, salt, pepper, thyme and nutmeg. Return to the heat and cook 1 minute. Slowly whisk in, or use a wooden spoon to stir in, the broth and milk. Cook over medium-low heat until slightly thickened. Stir in the Parmesan and Romano cheeses and sherry and cook 5 minutes, or until thickened.

Lightly butter a 9 x 13-inch baking dish and layer 4 of the noodles on the bottom. Cover with ½ the turkey, ½ the sliced mushrooms, ½ the mozzarella slices and ⅓ of the sauce. Repeat the layering, ending with the noodles topped with the sauce. Sprinkle with Parmesan cheese. Bake in a preheated 350-degree oven for 45 minutes. Serve with the cranberry sauce.

Serves 6.

Meat

Beef Burgundy
with Mixed Vegetables

*H*ere is an updated, and we think a healthier, version of a classic recipe.

2½ pounds beef stew meat, trimmed of fat and gristle and cut into 2-inch pieces
2 tablespoons olive oil
1 teaspoon salt, or to taste
½ teaspoon freshly ground pepper, or to taste
4 to 6 carrots, peeled and cut into 1-inch pieces
4 to 6 parsnips, peeled and cut into 1-inch pieces
5 leeks, thoroughly washed, all but 3 inches of green tops removed, cut into 3-inch pieces
1½ teaspoons granulated sugar
1½ cups good red wine, preferably a burgundy
1½ cups canned beef broth
2 tablespoons red currant jelly
1 teaspoon basil, crushed
1 teaspoon thyme
6 cloves garlic, minced
12 small new potatoes, red or wax variety, scrubbed and halved, or left whole if very small
1 16-ounce can Italian plum tomatoes, drained and coarsely chopped
¼ cup chopped parsley, for garnish

Heat olive oil in a large skillet and saute beef in small batches. Place browned meat in a heavy 5-quart casserole and sprinkle with salt and pepper. In the same skillet, lightly saute the carrots, parsnips and leeks. Sprinkle with the sugar and saute a minute longer. Remove to a separate bowl and set aside.

Add wine and beef broth to the skillet and scrape up any brown bits and bring to a boil. Reduce the heat and add the currant jelly, basil, thyme and garlic and simmer a few minutes. Pour over the beef and stir in the potatoes. Cover and bake in a preheated 350-degree oven for 45 minutes.

Remove casserole from the oven and stir in the carrots, parsnips, leeks and chopped tomatoes. Taste for salt and pepper and additional basil and thyme. Cover and return to oven for 30 minutes. Uncover and bake an additional 15 minutes. Sprinkle with parsley and serve.

Serves 6.

Baked Beef and Potato Stew

This casserole stew requires long, slow baking, but it is quickly assembled.

2½ pounds stewing beef, cut in 2-inch cubes
3 tablespoons olive oil
12 small new potatoes, scrubbed
1 16-ounce bag whole frozen onions
4 cloves garlic, minced
1 package dry onion soup mix
1 16-ounce can plum tomatoes, drained and chopped
1 cup beef broth
1 cup red wine
1 tablespoon soy sauce
1 bay leaf
1 teaspoon thyme
½ teaspoon salt, or more to taste
¼ teaspoon freshly ground pepper, or more to taste

In a flameproof 3-quart casserole with a cover, brown the beef in the olive oil; remove all but two tablespoons oil. Add rest of ingredients, mix well, and bring to boil on top of stove. Cover and bake in a 325-degree oven for 1½ to 2 hours until beef is fork tender; uncover casserole during last half hour of cooking to thicken sauce, if desired.

Serves 6.

Jumbo Shells with Beef and Cheese

This is a wonderful family casserole combining best-loved ingredients that freeze well. Make a double recipe, freeze half and dinner will be a snap at the end of one of those impossible days.

18 jumbo shells, cooked al dente
1½ pounds lean ground beef
1 onion, chopped
2 cloves garlic, minced
1 green pepper, cut into fine dice
1 teaspoon salt
½ teaspoon oregano
1 teaspoon basil
¼ teaspoon pepper

3 tablespoons olive oil
2 cloves garlic, minced
3 dried hot peppers
1 28-ounce can plum tomatoes, chopped, with their juice
1 egg, slightly beaten
1 pound mozzarella cheese, shredded
½ cup Parmesan cheese, shredded

Drain the cooked jumbo shells well and place in single layer on a cookie sheet. Set aside.

In a large frying pan, saute beef, onion, garlic, green pepper, salt, oregano, basil, and pepper until beef is no longer red. Set aside to cool.

To make the sauce, slowly saute the garlic and hot peppers in a saucepan in the olive oil until peppers are browned. Discard garlic and peppers. Carefully add the tomatoes to the oil, and simmer briskly about 20 minutes until sauce thickens. Stir frequently.

When meat mixture has cooled, mix in the beaten egg and half the shredded mozzarella. Stuff the reserved shells with the meat and cheese mixture.

In a 9 x 13-inch glass baking dish, spread about one cup of the tomato sauce. Arrange the stuffed shells in the dish, top with the remaining mozzarella and the rest of the tomato sauce. Sprinkle the Parmesan on top. Bake in a preheated 350-degree oven about 30 minutes or until cheese is bubbly and lightly browned.

Serves 6.

Beef and Beans with Beer

*B*eer is a classic accompaniment for slow-cooked beef casseroles and stews. Here we've speeded things up a bit by using canned beans and tenderizing the beef in the sauce on top of the stove, before combining it with the beans for a final bake.

2 pounds beef stew meat, excess fat and gristle removed
3 tablespoons olive oil
2 12-ounce cans beer
1 8-ounce bottle chili sauce
3 cloves garlic, minced
2 teaspoons sugar
½ teaspoon salt, or more to taste
¼ teaspoon freshly ground pepper, or more to taste
3 15-ounce cans small white beans, rinsed and drained
16-ounce bag tiny frozen onions
1 cup seasoned bread crumbs
Finely chopped parsley for garnish

In a 5-quart Dutch oven, brown the beef in the olive oil in small batches so beef browns and does not steam. Add beer, chili sauce, garlic, sugar, salt and pepper to pan, bring to boil, then reduce to a simmer. Simmer, uncovered, for 30 minutes or until beef is tender.

Preheat oven to 375 degrees. Add beans and onions to Dutch oven, stir and bring to boil. If mixture is very soupy, reduce sauce by boiling for several minutes. Sprinkle bread crumbs on top of mixture and place in oven, uncovered; bake for about 30 minutes or until casserole is bubbly and bread crumbs lightly browned. Sprinkle with parsley and serve from casserole.

Serves 6.

Oven Chili

E veryone has a favorite chili recipe, it seems. This one bubbles away merrily in the oven while you fix the accompaniments: diced raw onions, shredded sharp cheddar cheese, sour cream and sliced black olives. Forget what the purists say—this is delicious.

2 pounds lean ground beef
1 large onion, chopped
3 cloves garlic, minced
2 tablespoons oil for browning meat, if it is very lean
3 tablespoons chili powder
1 tablespoon cumin
1 teaspoon oregano
1 tablespoon dry mustard
¼ teaspoon cayenne pepper
1 tablespoon salt, or to taste
3 15-ounce cans small white beans, such as Great Northern, rinsed and drained
1 28-ounce can cooking tomatoes, chopped, with juice

In a large flameproof casserole, saute the beef, onion, and garlic in oil, stirring until beef is no longer red. Drain off all but about 2 tablespoons oil. Stir the dry seasonings into the beef mixture. Stir while cooking over moderate heat for about 2 minutes. Add the beans and tomatoes, stir, and bring to a boil. Cover and place in preheated 375-degree oven for about 30 minutes. Stir once during the baking. If chili seems dry, add a little beef broth; if it is too soupy, remove cover during baking.

Serves 6.

The Kids' Night Casserole

This is definitely for the family that shares the cooking. Be sure to take the meat out of the freezer in the a.m. Have salad fixings available or serve sliced fresh fruit. In a pinch, chilled canned fruit packed in its own juice will do.

1 cup rice, uncooked
1 cup frozen peas
½ cup chopped onion
½ cup chopped red or green pepper
1 clove garlic, minced (or more to taste)
1 8-ounce can tomato sauce
1½ pounds lean ground beef or 1½ pounds ground turkey
1 teaspoon seasoned salt (plain is okay too)
¼ teaspoon ground pepper
1 teaspoon oregano, crushed
1 16-ounce can tomatoes, coarsely chopped, juice drained and added to water
   to make ½ cup liquid
1 cup grated sharp cheddar cheese (optional)

Preheat oven to 350 degrees.

Layer all the ingredients in a 2-quart casserole in the order given. If cheese is not used, sprinkle top layer with additional salt. Cover with foil and bake for 1 hour. Carefully remove foil, stir gently and bake an additional 15 minutes.

Serves 6.

Family Favorite Hamburger Casserole

This is another kids' favorite, either prepared by them or by other family members. We hope your family enjoys it too. You might like to pass bowls of salsa and sour cream and a basket of warm, crisp tortilla chips as accompaniments.

2 tablespoons olive oil
1 large onion, chopped
1½ pounds lean ground beef
1 teaspoon salt
2½ cups broken medium egg noodles (uncooked)
1 28-ounce can tomatoes, not drained and tomatoes coarsely chopped
½ cup catsup
¾ cup water
2 tablespoons Worcestershire sauce
1 8-ounce can corn, drained
½ teaspoon seasoned salt
1 4-ounce can chopped green chilies
1 small can chopped ripe olives
½ cup freshly grated Parmesan cheese
1 cup shredded sharp cheddar cheese
Paprika

Heat oil in a large skillet and add onions, ground beef, salt, noodles and tomatoes. Cover and cook over medium heat for 15 minutes. Transfer to a 3-quart casserole. Stir in catsup, water, Worcestershire sauce, corn, seasoned salt, green chilies, olives, and Parmesan cheese. Top with cheddar cheese and sprinkle with paprika.

Bake, covered, in a preheated 350-degree oven for 45 minutes. Turn off oven heat, uncover and let stand in the oven for 15 minutes.

Serves 6.

Tortilla Pie

Accompany this soul-satisfying dish with an avocado, orange and lettuce salad topped with cucumber and pineapple salsa. Pass a bowl of tomato salsa to garnish the pie.

Tortilla Pie Shell
1 package dry pie crust mix
½ teaspoon chili powder
½ teaspoon cumin seeds
½ teaspoon ground coriander
Pinch of cayenne pepper

Meat and Zucchini Filling
1 pound lean ground beef
½ cup chopped onion
1 clove garlic, minced
1 teaspoon basil, crushed, or 1 tablespoon fresh basil, shredded
1 teaspoon oregano, crushed
¼ teaspoon dried red pepper flakes
½ teaspoon salt
2 eggs, lightly beaten
1½ pounds zucchini, scrubbed and coarsely shredded, excess moisture patted off
  between layers of paper toweling
1 cup low-fat cottage cheese
1 cup shredded sharp cheddar cheese
3 tablespoons chopped parsley, or cilantro if available
1 4-ounce can chopped green chilies
1 teaspoon Worcestershire sauce
1 teaspoon dry mustard

In a medium bowl, mix dry ingredients together, then proceed with directions on the package to make dough. Roll out dough (not too thin) to a 12-inch circle and fit into a deep 9-inch pie plate, crimping the edges.

Brown meat with onions and garlic. Stir in basil, oregano, red pepper flakes and salt. Set aside.

In a medium-sized bowl, beat eggs and stir in zucchini, cottage cheese, cheddar cheese, parsley, green chilies, Worcestershire sauce, dry mustard and salt to taste.

Spoon meat mixture into pie shell and top with the zucchini and cheese mixture. Bake in preheated 350-degree oven for 45 minutes. Cool 10 minutes and cut into wedges to serve.

Serves 6.

Curried Shepherd's Pie Casserole

*I*n addition to updating this classic dish with curry and other spices, we are simplifying by using instant, but good quality, potato flakes, such as Pillsbury or Betty Crocker. You can also replace the ground beef with ground turkey.

1 cup chopped onions
2 tablespoons olive oil
1 tablespoon curry powder
1 teaspoon ground coriander
1 teaspoon ground cumin
Seeds from 3 cardamom pods, or ½ teaspoon ground cardamom
2 pounds lean ground beef or ground turkey
1½ teaspoons salt
¼ teaspoon pepper
1 16-ounce can whole plum tomatoes, drained and coarsely chopped
1½ cups diced carrots
½ cup canned beef broth
1 10-ounce package frozen peas, blanched under running hot water
6 servings of instant mashed potatoes, prepared according to package directions
2 tablespoons margarine or butter

Heat oil in a large skillet and saute onions until limp and golden. Reduce heat and stir in curry powder, coriander, cumin and cardamom. Heat through until fragrant. Add ground beef and cook over higher heat until nicely browned. Stir in salt, pepper, tomatoes, diced carrots and beef broth. Simmer for 30 minutes, stirring occasionally. Stir in blanched peas and remove from the heat.

Prepare the potatoes while the meat mixture simmers.

To assemble casserole, transfer the meat mixture to a 3-quart casserole dish. Carefully spread the mashed potatoes on top and dot with butter or margarine. Preheat the broiler and run the casserole under the broiler until the butter melts and the potatoes brown slightly.

Serves 6.

Touch of the Irish Casserole

*W*e *highly recommend a large loaf of Irish soda bread to sop up the slightly heady sauce.*

2½ pounds beef stew meat, trimmed of excess fat and gristle and cut into 1½-inch pieces
½ cup flour, mixed with 1½ teaspoons salt and ½ teaspoon pepper
3 tablespoons olive oil, divided
4 cups sliced onions
4 cloves garlic, minced
8 medium potatoes, peeled and cut into quarters
1 12-ounce bottle Guinness Stout
1 12-ounce bottle Harp or other full-bodied beer
1 cup beef broth
Bouquet garni: 8 sprigs parsley, 8 peppercorns, 1 teaspoon thyme, 2 bay leaves,
    1 teaspoon dill seeds, 4 whole cloves; all tied together in cheesecloth
3 tablespoons brown sugar
1 tablespoon horseradish

Toss the stew meat with the flour mixture. Brown small batches of the meat in hot oil in a 3-quart Dutch oven. Remove with a slotted spoon to a plate.

Add 1 tablespoon oil and, when hot, stir in the onions and saute until limp and golden. Add the garlic and cook 1 minute. Return the meat to the Dutch oven and add potatoes, stout, beer, beef broth, bouquet garni, brown sugar and horseradish. Bring to a boil, cover tightly and bake in a preheated 325-degree oven for 2½ hours. Remove bouquet garni and serve.

Serves 6.

Old Athens Meat and Spinach "Pie"

This is a combination of some of our favorite Greek dishes. You might like to precede the "pie" with Avgolemono Soup (Greek egg-and-lemon soup).

Pastry
½ pound phyllo leaves
1 stick margarine, melted (or, for the non-cholesterol conscious, use all butter or half margarine and half butter)

Meat Layer
1½ cups coarsely chopped onions
2 tablespoons olive oil
2 cloves garlic, minced
1½ pounds lean ground beef (or ground lamb)
1 teaspoon salt
½ teaspoon pepper
1 teaspoon oregano, crushed
½ teaspoon ground cinnamon
½ cup tomato paste

Spinach and Cheese Layer
6 green onions, sliced in ½-inch pieces
1 tablespoon olive oil
2 packages frozen chopped spinach, briefly cooked and excess water squeezed out
½ cup chopped fresh dill or 3 teaspoons dried dillweed
½ cup chopped parsley
¼ cup chopped fresh mint (do not use dried mint)
1 teaspoon salt (or more to taste after cheeses are added)
½ teaspoon pepper
2 eggs, lightly beaten
½ pound feta cheese, crumbled
1 cup low-fat cottage or ricotta cheese

Brush a 3-quart round glass casserole dish with some of the melted margarine and set aside.

In a skillet, saute the chopped onions in 2 tablespoons oil until limp and slightly golden; add the garlic and saute briefly. Add the ground beef, raise the heat and cook until well browned. Add the remaining meat layer ingredients and mix well. Set aside.

Saute the green onions in 1 tablespoon oil until soft. Stir in the cooked spinach, dill, parsley, mint, salt and pepper and cook briefly. Remove from the heat and mix in the eggs and cheeses. Set aside.

Unroll phyllo leaves and keep covered with a slightly damp cloth to prevent them from drying out. Layer the bottom of the casserole dish with 6 leaves of pastry, brushing each leaf with melted margarine. Spread meat mixture over the pastry. Spread spinach and cheese mixture over meat. Top with remaining pastry, again brushing each leaf with melted margarine. Tuck overhanging pastry inside casserole. Brush top with melted margarine and score through pastry with a sharp knife into serving-size wedges.

Serves 6.

Picadillo

For a true Latin meal, serve this sweet and hot ground beef casserole over rice and, if you're not watching your cholesterol, with a fried egg on each serving. Sauteed ripe plantains make an interesting accompaniment.

2½ pounds lean ground beef
½ teaspoon salt, or more to taste
¼ teaspoon freshly ground pepper, or more to taste
1 large onion, diced
1 red or green pepper, diced
2 cloves garlic, diced
1 16-ounce can plum tomatoes, chopped in can with a long knife
1 tablespoon wine vinegar
½ teaspoon hot pepper flakes, or to taste
1 bay leaf
12 stuffed olives, halved
½ cup raisins
½ cup slivered almonds, browned in oil or butter

Season beef with salt and pepper and brown it in a frying pan; drain well and set aside. In a flameproof 2-quart casserole, saute onions, pepper and garlic in the olive oil until onion is soft. Add remaining ingredients and ground beef to the casserole, bring to boil, cover and bake in 375-degree oven for 25 minutes. Remove bay leaf and serve.

Serves 6.

Eggplant, Rice and Ground Beef Casserole

Did you know eggplant is good for you? Jean Carper, a well-known writer on health and nutrition, tells us that studies show eggplant helps protect arteries and can help lower blood cholesterol. It even has some properties that fight the effects of saturated fats in meat. To make an even healthier casserole, you can substitute ground turkey for the beef.

1 large eggplant, peeled and cut crosswise into ½-inch slices
3 tablespoons olive oil
1½ pounds lean ground beef or turkey
½ cup chopped onion
2 cloves garlic, minced
¼ cup chopped parsley
1 teaspoon oregano, crushed
½ teaspoon marjoram, crushed
1 teaspoon salt
¼ teaspoon pepper
Pinch of red pepper flakes
¾ cup raw white or brown rice, cooked according to package directions
3 cups canned stewed tomatoes

Lay the eggplant slices on a piece of waxed paper or plastic wrap and sprinkle with salt. (This helps remove any bitter taste.) After 15 minutes, rinse the eggplant and pat it dry. Heat oil in a large skillet and lightly saute the eggplant (don't let it get too soft). Set aside on paper toweling.

Mix together ground meat, onion, garlic, parsley, oregano, marjoram, salt, pepper and red pepper flakes. In a lightly-oiled 2½ or 3-quart casserole, layer half the eggplant, half the rice, half the meat mixture and half the stewed tomatoes. Repeat the layering, ending with tomatoes.

Bake in a preheated 350-degree oven, uncovered, for 45 minutes.

Serves 6.

Indian Beef and Vegetable Casserole

I ndian spices add a wonderful aroma and flavor to a standard beef, carrot and potato combination. This is a "dry" casserole, uncovered for the last half of the cooking so the edges of the meat and potatoes can get a little crispy.

3 pounds beef stew meat, cut into 1½-inch cubes
Flour seasoned with salt and pepper
3–4 tablespoons vegetable oil
1 onion, chopped
2 cloves garlic, minced
12 small boiling potatoes, scrubbed and halved
8 carrots, scraped and cut into 2-inch pieces
1 teaspoon curry powder
1 teaspoon ground cumin
1 teaspoon turmeric
1 teaspoon ground coriander
½ teaspoon ground cinnamon
½ teaspoon ground ginger
½ teaspoon dry mustard
¼ teaspoon black pepper
¼ teaspoon red pepper
½ teaspoon salt
1½ cups beef broth

Coat beef cubes with the seasoned flour. In a flameproof 3-quart casserole with a lid, brown the beef in batches in the oil. Remove and set aside. Saute onion and garlic in the oil until onion is translucent. Add beef, potatoes and carrots to the casserole.

In a small bowl, mix together the dry spices and seasonings. Sprinkle over meat and vegetables, stir well and cook over moderate heat for a few minutes until seasonings are aromatic. Add broth, bring to boil, and place in a preheated 350-degree oven. Cover casserole. Bake 45 minutes, then remove cover and continue baking until vegetables and meat are tender, about ½ hour. There should be very little liquid left in the casserole, but if dish dries out during baking, add a little more broth.

Serves 6.

Fruited Beef Casserole

Dried fruit and meat make a delicious combination. In this easy oven stew, the sauce has a touch of heat to balance the sweetness. Serve with rice.

1 10-ounce package of mixed dried fruit
Hot water to cover fruit, about 1 cup
2½ pounds stewing beef, cut into 1-inch pieces with excess fat and gristle removed
3 tablespoons olive oil
Flour seasoned with salt and pepper
1 medium onion, chopped
3 cloves garlic, minced
1 large carrot, scraped and diced
1 cup beef broth
½ teaspoon Italian seasoning
1 teaspoon Tabasco-type sauce, or to taste
1 cup dry red wine
½ teaspoon salt, or more to taste
¼ teaspoon freshly ground pepper, or more to taste
1 tablespoon instant-blending flour

Halve or quarter large pieces of the dried fruit. Place in a bowl and cover with hot water; set aside.

Toss beef cubes in the seasoned flour. In a 3-quart Dutch oven or flameproof casserole, brown the floured beef in the olive oil. Remove and set aside. Saute the onion, garlic and carrots in the oil until onion is translucent. Return beef to pan, and add rest of ingredients except dried fruit.

Bring mixture to boil on top of stove, then bake, covered, for 45 minutes in a 350-degree oven. Add fruit and the fruit water, recover and bake an additional 30 minutes. If sauce needs to be thickened, sprinkle on about 1 tablespoon instant-blending flour, stir, and continue baking about 15 minutes.

Serves 6.

Beef and Noodle Paprikash

T his has been a family favorite for years and a cook's favorite too, because it is so easy. Plan a side dish of vegetables and either a basket of biscuits or hearty bread to sop up the extra sauce.

2½ pounds beef stew meat, trimmed of fat and gristle, left in large pieces
2 tablespoons olive oil
2 large onions, coarsely chopped
2 cloves garlic, minced
2 teaspoons sweet Hungarian paprika
1½ teaspoons salt
Pinch of cayenne pepper, about ⅛ teaspoon
1 teaspoon basil, crushed
Hot water and juice from tomatoes to equal 2 cups
1 8-ounce can tomato sauce
1 16-ounce can tomatoes, drained and chopped (juice reserved)
½ pound wide egg noodles, slightly broken
½ cup sour cream, optional
3 tablespoons chopped parsley, for garnish

Heat oil in a heavy 3-quart casserole and brown meat in small batches. Add the onions to the last batch and brown with the meat. Add the reserved browned meat and any accumulated juices, the garlic, paprika, salt, cayenne pepper, basil, water, tomato sauce and tomatoes. Stir together and simmer on top of the stove 1½ hours; stir occasionally.

Stir in the noodles, cover and cook about 15 minutes more or until the noodles are done. If desired, stir in the sour cream just before serving and sprinkle with chopped parsley.

Serves 6.

Ersatz Sauerbraten

This version of the classic German stew has all the taste elements, but eliminates the long marinating step and uses stew meat instead of a single piece of chuck or rump roast. We also digress from the original by cooking the potatoes and carrots with the meat.

2½ pounds beef stew meat, trimmed of excess fat and gristle and cut into 1½-inch pieces
3 tablespoons olive oil, divided
1½ cups sliced onions
2 cups hot water
1 cup dry red wine
2 teaspoons salt
½ teaspoon pepper
3 teaspoons caraway seeds
2 bay leaves
½ cup white vinegar
5 medium potatoes, peeled and cut into 1½-inch cubes
4 medium carrots, peeled and cut into 1-inch pieces
½ cup coarsely crushed gingersnaps
⅓ cup water

Heat 2 tablespoons oil in a 5-quart Dutch oven and brown stew meat in small batches. Set browned meat aside; saute the onions in 1 tablespoon oil until limp and lightly golden. Stir in hot water, wine, salt, pepper, caraway seeds, bay leaves and browned meat. Bring to a boil, cover, reduce heat and simmer 1½ hours. Stir meat, add vinegar, potatoes and carrots and simmer 45 minutes.

In a small bowl, combine gingersnap crumbs with ⅓ cup water. Stir into hot stew and simmer, uncovered, a few minutes until slightly thickened and heated through.

Serves 6.

Classic Cholent

*T*his *long-cooking casserole of the meat-and-bean family is a tradition of Eastern European Jewish communities. There are dozens of variations from family to family, but all agree cholent tastes better on the second day, or third, if it lasts that long. This version serves 10 ("no sense making less," the author of the recipe suggests).*

1½ pounds dried large white lima beans or Great Northern beans
1½ cups barley
3 large onions, thickly sliced
3 large cloves garlic, chunked
5–6 pieces beef marrow bone, including both end pieces and shaft piece containing marrow (order from butcher)
Oil for browning meat
1 pound beef stew meat in 1½-inch chunks (brisket or flank cuts are ideal)
2 pounds beef short ribs
1½ tablespoons coarse or Kosher salt
1–2 tablespoons paprika, depending on freshness
1 teaspoon freshly ground black pepper
2 tablespoons flour

Four hours before preparing the casserole, place the beans in a large bowl and cover them with at least 1 inch of boiling water. Set aside to soak.

When soaking of beans is nearly complete, heat 1 to 2 tablespoons oil (chicken fat is traditional) in a heavy 8-quart pot with a lid. Brown the stew meat and ribs over high heat in small batches to prevent steaming. Remove from the pot and set aside. Discard the fat from the pot, leaving behind the meat juices and bits of meat on the bottom of the pot. Add the onions and garlic and cook over high heat, stirring occasionally, until browned, about 5–6 minutes. Lower the heat and add the marrow bones, coarse salt, black pepper and paprika, stir and cook about 5 minutes.

Add stew meat, short ribs, the drained beans and barley to the pot. Sprinkle the flour on top and stir once. Pour boiling water over all to cover.

Bring the pot to a boil on top of the stove, cover tightly and transfer to the middle rack of the oven. Cook 35 minutes at 375 degrees, then lower the heat to 250 degrees. Leave in a slow oven overnight or 12–16 hours. Do not stir during cooking.

When cooking is complete, make a well in the surface of the cholent with the back of a large spoon. If any fat accumulates in the well, spoon it off and discard; repeat as necessary.

Serves 10.

Beef and Barley in a Pot

The people of Eastern Europe have long used barley as a staple in their diets, primarily because it was inexpensive. Scientists now say it is as effective as oats in lowering blood cholesterol. It also makes a wonderfully hearty meal as prepared here.

2½ pounds beef stew meat, trimmed of excess fat and gristle and cut into 1½-inch pieces
2 tablespoons olive oil
1½ cups chopped onion
2 cloves garlic, minced
1 medium green pepper, sliced into ¼-inch strips
1 28-ounce can whole tomatoes, undrained and crushed
4 large carrots, peeled and cut into 1-inch pieces
1 cup barley
2 cups hot water
¼ cup chopped parsley
1 teaspoon basil, crushed
½ teaspoon thyme
2 teaspoons caraway seeds
1½ teaspoons salt
½ teaspoon pepper

Heat oil in a 4-quart Dutch oven. Brown meat in batches and remove to a bowl. Add onions to the pot and saute until lightly browned. Add garlic for the last minute of sauteing.

Return meat to the pot and stir in peppers, tomatoes, carrots, water, barley, parsley, basil, thyme, caraway seeds, salt and pepper. Bring to a boil, reduce heat, cover and cook 1 hour or until meat and barley and carrots are tender. Stir occasionally and taste for seasoning; adjust if necessary.

Serves 6.

Tzimmes: A Beef, Sweet Potato, Carrot and Dried Fruit Casserole

*T*zimmes are Eastern European in origin. The word means, roughly, "to make a fuss over or lavish attention on," but the most familiar translation is "a good-for-you stew." Like ethnic dishes of every culture, there are numerous recipes for tzimmes. Many are made without meat and served as a side dish; all taste better if made at least the day before serving.

3 pounds beef stew meat, trimmed of excess fat and gristle and left in large pieces
2 tablespoons olive oil
1 cup coarsely chopped onions
1½ cups hot water
1½ teaspoons salt
½ teaspoon pepper
1 bay leaf
6 carrots peeled and cut into 1-inch pieces
2 medium sweet potatoes, peeled and cut into large cubes
½ pound pitted prunes
½ pound dried apricots
¼ cup honey
2 tablespoons lemon juice
Juice of ½ orange
1 4-inch piece cinnamon stick, or 1 teaspoon ground cinnamon
1 teaspoon thyme

Heat oil in a 4 or 5-quart Dutch oven, add the stew meat in small batches and brown well on all sides. Set the browned meat aside, add the onions and saute until almost brown. Return the meat to the pot, add the water, salt, pepper and bay leaf and bring to a boil. Cover tightly, place in a preheated 350-degree oven and cook 1 hour.

Reduce the heat to 325 degrees. Stir remaining ingredients into the meat. Cover and continue baking for 2 hours. After the first hour add some hot water or beef broth if the casserole seems to be drying out.

Serves 6.

California Veal and Mushroom Casserole

*T*his casserole has some unexpected and subtle flavors that make it a perfect company dish, but there's no reason why your family shouldn't be treated like company occasionally.

2½ pounds veal stew meat, cut into 2-inch cubes
2 tablespoons olive oil, divided
2 tablespoons butter, divided
3 tablespoons flour
1½ teaspoons sweet Hungarian paprika
1½ teaspoons ground coriander
1½ teaspoons salt
¼ teaspoon freshly ground pepper
1 16-ounce can plum tomatoes, coarsely chopped, not drained
¼ cup oil-packed sun-dried tomatoes, chopped, or the dry-packed variety reconstituted as package directs
1½ cups hot chicken broth
1½ cups thinly sliced onions
3 cloves garlic, minced
¼ cup chopped cilantro, or parsley
1 tablespoon chopped fresh tarragon, or 1½ teaspoons dried tarragon, crushed
Grated rind of one large orange
¾ cup raw rice, sauteed in 1 tablespoon butter
½ pound mushrooms, preferably a wild variety, either halved, quartered or sliced depending on the variety
1 tablespoon butter
1 cup coarsely chopped fresh tomatoes
Orange strips, for garnish

Heat 1 tablespoon oil and 1 tablespoon butter over high heat in a 4-quart Dutch oven and brown the veal in small batches. Do not crowd the meat or it will steam and not brown. Add oil and butter as needed to brown all the meat.

In a small bowl, mix together the flour, paprika, coriander, salt and pepper. Return all the meat and any accumulated juices to the casserole and sprinkle the flour mixture on top. Stir gently into the meat and cook over low heat for 2 to 3 minutes. Add the chopped plum tomatoes, sun-dried tomatoes, chicken broth, onions, garlic, cilantro or parsley, tarragon, orange rind and sauteed rice. Mix well, cover and bake in a preheated 350-degree oven for 1 hour.

While the casserole is baking, melt the remaining tablespoon of butter and saute the mushrooms over high heat until golden or lightly browned, depending on the type of mushroom used.

After 1 hour, gently stir the sauteed mushrooms and the chopped fresh tomatoes into the casserole. Cover, return to the oven and continue baking for an additional 15 minutes. Garnish with the orange strips and serve.

Serves 6.

Veal and Pasta with Gremolata

*T*o *pursue an Italian theme for your menu, try a first course of chilled canned white beans and sauteed onions with chopped fresh sage, crunchy Italian bread and a sinful tira misu for dessert.*

2½ pounds veal stew meat, cut into 2-inch cubes
½ cup flour mixed with 1 teaspoon salt, ½ teaspoon freshly ground pepper
    and ½ teaspoon ground sage
2 tablespoons olive oil
1 cup coarsely chopped onions
3 carrots, peeled and sliced into ½-inch pieces
3 stalks celery, sliced
1½ cups chicken broth
½ cup dry white wine
¼ cup tomato paste
2 teaspoons fresh rosemary, chopped, or 1 teaspoon dried rosemary, crushed
3 cups cooked pasta, rotini, rotelle or any short tube shape, cooked al dente
1 10-ounce package frozen tiny peas, thawed and drained

Gremolata
Grated rind of 2 lemons
⅓ cup finely chopped parsley
1 teaspoon minced garlic

Toss the veal cubes in the seasoned flour. In a 4-quart Dutch oven, brown meat in oil in small batches. Set meat aside.

Saute onions, carrots and celery in the casserole until onion is soft. Stir in chicken broth, wine, tomato paste and rosemary and simmer about 3 minutes.

Return the veal to the casserole, add the pasta and stir together. Cover and bake in a preheated 350-degree oven for 1 hour. Stir in the peas and bake an additional 10 minutes.

Combine the lemon rind, parsley and garlic and set aside. Stir the gremolata into the casserole at the table to enjoy the full effect of its fragrance.

Serves 6.

Veal or Turkey Sausages with Rice and Olives

*Y*ou *might like to serve this casserole with your favorite corn bread or, for a change, try crispy corn cakes made with lots of whole kernels of corn.*

2 pounds veal or turkey sausage links
Olive oil
2 cups chopped onion
1 cup chopped green pepper
1 cup chopped red or yellow pepper
1¼ cups raw rice
2 teaspoons chili powder
1 teaspoon fennel seeds
3 cups chicken broth
1 cup pimento-stuffed small olives, halved
¼ cup minced cilantro or parsley

Brown the sausages over low heat in a large skillet. Remove to a plate to cool, then slice in ½-inch rounds.

Add olive oil to the drippings in the pan to equal 2 tablespoons. Stir in the onions and peppers and cook until slightly soft. Stir in the rice and saute until golden. Stir in chili powder and fennel and saute 1 minute more. Add chicken broth and bring to a boil. Stir in sliced sausage and olives and transfer to a 2 or 3-quart casserole.

Bake in a preheated 375-degree oven for 45 minutes or until the rice is cooked. Fluff the rice once during baking. Sprinkle with the chopped cilantro or parsley before serving.

Serves 6.

All-American Lamb and Potatoes

*W*e think you will like this variation on a basic meat-and-potatoes combination. For color and texture contrast, serve with ultra-healthy lightly steamed broccoli.

2½ pounds boneless lamb, trimmed and cut in 2-inch cubes
2 tablespoons olive oil, divided
1 tablespoon margarine or butter
3 medium onions, sliced
2 cloves garlic, minced
1 10-ounce can beef broth
1 teaspoon rosemary, divided
½ teaspoon thyme
½ teaspoon salt
¼ teaspoon pepper, or more to taste
6 medium potatoes, peeled and sliced about ¼-inch thick

In a large skillet, heat 1 tablespoon oil over high heat and brown half of the lamb cubes. Remove with a slotted spoon, add more oil if needed, and brown the remaining meat and set aside.

Add the 1 tablespoon margarine or butter to the skillet and saute the onions over medium heat until limp and golden. Add the garlic and saute for 2 minutes. Add broth, ½ teaspoon rosemary, thyme, ½ teaspoon salt and ¼ teaspoon pepper and bring to a boil.

Place sliced potatoes in the bottom of a 3-quart casserole, pour onion and broth mixture over, then top with the lamb cubes. Sprinkle the lamb with additional salt and pepper and ½ teaspoon rosemary.

Cover and bake in a preheated 350-degree oven for 1 hour. Spoon the broth over the meat once or twice during baking.

This dish can also be cooked over low heat on top of the stove. Use a flameproof casserole, or layer sliced potatoes on the bottom of the skillet used for sauteing, with onion mixture and meat on top. Cook covered.

Serves 6.

Persian Bulgur Wheat and Lamb Casserole

*B*ulgur *is as much a staple of Middle Eastern cooking as it is in Eastern Europe. The additions of split peas, pasta, mint and cinnamon recall an Iranian dish called Ahsh.*

½ cup dried yellow split peas, soaked overnight in cold water or parboiled for 30 minutes and drained
4 cups chicken broth, or more as needed
1 pound ground lamb
¼ cup minced onion
1 large clove garlic, minced
½ teaspoon salt
¼ teaspoon pepper
½ teaspoon ground cinnamon
3 carrots, peeled and cut into 1-inch pieces
¾ cup bulgur wheat
1 cup short lengths of thin spaghetti
½ cup chopped parsley
6 green onions, chopped
2 tablespoons chopped fresh mint (do not use dried mint; eliminate if not available)
½ cup golden raisins

Heat chicken broth in a 3-quart saucepan or flameproof casserole. Stir in drained peas. Bring to a boil, cover, reduce heat and simmer 20 minutes.

Mix together ground lamb, onion, garlic, salt, pepper and cinnamon. Shape into small 1½-inch balls and brown in a non-stick skillet, or with 1 tablespoon olive oil in a regular skillet. Set aside.

Add the carrots and bulgur to the simmering broth and peas and cook, covered, 30 minutes. Stir in the lamb, spaghetti, parsley, green onions, mint and raisins and cook, uncovered, 10 minutes.

Serves 6.

Lamb Casserole with Easy Puff Pastry

*D*o not be deterred by the number of steps needed to complete this very tasty dish, as most of the casserole can be prepared a day or two in advance of serving. A chilled orange or lemon souffle or mousse would be an appropriate dessert for this rather rich entree.

½ cup flour mixed with 1 teaspoon salt, ½ teaspoon pepper and ½ teaspoon thyme

2½ pounds boneless leg of lamb, trimmed and cut into 1½-inch cubes

3 tablespoons olive oil, divided

3 tablespoons butter, divided

4 leeks, trimmed of green leaves, white part split lengthwise, rinsed well and thinly sliced

2 cloves garlic, minced

1 tablespoon flour

1½ cups dry red wine

1 bay leaf, crumbled

2 tablespoons tomato paste

3 tablespoons chopped parsley

2 teaspoons chopped fresh rosemary, or 1 teaspoon dried, crushed

2 cups beef broth

½ cup dry sherry

1 tablespoon red currant jelly

½ teaspoon salt, or to taste

¼ teaspoon pepper

4 medium turnips peeled and cut into 1-inch cubes, or use white potatoes if preferred

3 large carrots, peeled, quartered and cut into 3-inch lengths

1 10-ounce box frozen pearl onions, thawed

2 tablespoons butter

½ pound green beans, tipped and cut into halves or thirds

12 large mushrooms, cleaned and quartered

1 teaspoon sugar

Pinch of freshly ground pepper

3 medium tomatoes, seeded and quartered

Half of a 10-ounce package frozen tiny green peas

3 tablespoons chopped parsley

1 package frozen puff pastry

1 egg, beaten with 1 teaspoon cold water

Toss the cubed lamb in the seasoned flour. In a large skillet, heat 2 tablespoons oil and 1 tablespoon butter over medium-high heat and brown the lamb in small batches; remove with a slotted spoon.

Heat 1 tablespoon oil and 2 tablespoons butter in the skillet over medium heat and saute the leeks and garlic about 2 minutes. Sprinkle with 1 tablespoon flour, stir and cook 1 minute. Pour in the red wine, stirring up any browned bits, and cook over high heat until reduced by half. Remove from the heat and stir in bay leaf, tomato paste, parsley, rosemary, beef broth, sherry and jelly. Season with ½ teaspoon salt and ¼ teaspoon pepper and return lamb to the skillet. Reduce heat, cover and simmer 1 hour.

At this point the meat can be cooled, covered and refrigerated for 1 day before proceeding. Reheat slowly before continuing.

While meat is simmering, bring a large saucepan of salted water to a boil. Add the turnips or potatoes and cook 3 minutes; remove with a slotted spoon. Add carrots and cook 5 minutes, then add thawed pearl onions and immediately drain both carrots and onions. Drain all vegetables thoroughly.

Melt remaining 2 tablespoons butter in the large saucepan and add cooked turnips, carrots, onions and green beans, mushrooms, sugar and pepper. Stir constantly about 3 minutes or until all vegetables are glazed with the butter and sugar.

Transfer the lamb mixture to a flameproof 3 or 4-quart casserole and carefully mix in the glazed vegetables. Cover and simmer 30 minutes.

The casserole can be refrigerated at this point for up to 2 days. Bring to room temperature, then add the quartered tomatoes and parsley. Cook over a low heat about 20 minutes.

Prepare the puff pastry as the package directs; roll it out to about ¼-inch thickness to fit the casserole. Brush the edge of the casserole with the beaten egg and lay the pastry on top; trim the excess and set aside for decorations. Crimp the pastry to the edge of the casserole to seal. Cut leaves or other decorations from the remaining pastry, brush the casserole with the egg wash and apply the decorations. Cut a steam hole in the center of the casserole with a sharp knife. Insert a small tube of foil in the hole so it doesn't close while baking. Bake in a 425-degree oven for 30 minutes or until the pastry is browned. Serve immediately.

Serves 6.

Lamb with Lentils and Dill

The lentils in this casserole will have a rather smooth texture after baking, so we suggest crisply cooked green beans with lightly sauteed peppers as a side dish. A fresh fruit compote with sugar cookies makes a light dessert.

2½ pounds boneless leg or shoulder of lamb, trimmed and cut into 2-inch cubes and patted dry with paper toweling

2 cloves garlic, crushed

3 tablespoons olive oil, divided

1 teaspoon rosemary, crushed

½ teaspoon salt, or more to taste

¼ teaspoon freshly ground pepper, or more to taste

1½ cups thinly sliced onions

4 cloves garlic, minced

1½ cups lentils, rinsed and picked over

¼ cup lemon juice

Grated rind from 1 lemon

¼ cup chopped fresh dill, or 1 tablespoon dried dillweed

3 cups beef broth, heated (or more if needed)

Salt and pepper to taste

3 tablespoons chopped parsley and 1 teaspoon grated lemon rind, mixed, for garnish

In a 3-quart Dutch oven, heat 2 tablespoons oil and 2 crushed garlic cloves over medium heat until the garlic begins to color; remove garlic and discard. Raise the heat to high and brown the cubed lamb in small batches. Sprinkle with rosemary, salt and pepper and set aside.

Add 1 tablespoon oil to the Dutch oven or skillet and saute onions until limp; add the garlic and cook 2 minutes.

Return the lamb and any accumulated juices to the pot; top with the lentils, lemon juice and rind, chopped dill and hot beef broth. Cover and bake in a preheated 350-degree oven for 2 hours. After 1 hour, gently stir ingredients together. Taste for salt and pepper and stir in additional hot broth as needed to cook lentils. Before serving, sprinkle with the parsley and lemon rind mixture.

Serves 6.

Moroccan Lamb and Couscous Casserole

*Y*ou *might like to serve lightly chilled stuffed grape leaves and a variety of ripe and green olives as an appetizer for this Moroccan dinner. With the casserole, we suggest herb-buttered toasted pita bread and ratatouille.*

2½ pounds boneless leg of lamb, cut into 2-inch cubes
⅓ cup flour mixed with 1 teaspoon salt, ½ teaspoon pepper and ½ teaspoon thyme
4 tablespoons olive oil, divided
2 large red or green peppers, thinly sliced
2 large onions, halved and sliced
4 cloves garlic, minced
½ teaspoon ground ginger
1 teaspoon ground cinnamon
½ teaspoon ground cumin
½ teaspoon ground coriander
½ teaspoon ground cardamom
¼ teaspoon red pepper flakes
3 cups beef broth
3 tablespoons tomato paste
1 cup quick-cook couscous
1 cup golden raisins
½ cup sliced almonds, lightly toasted
½ cup small pimento-stuffed olives

Toss cubed lamb in the seasoned flour. Heat 2 tablespoons oil in a 4-quart Dutch oven and brown the meat in batches. As meat browns, remove with a slotted spoon and set aside.

Add remaining oil to the pot and saute the peppers until they wilt; remove with a slotted spoon and set aside. Add the onions and saute until limp and golden; add the garlic and cook another 2 minutes. Stir in the ginger, cinnamon, cumin, coriander, cardamom and pepper flakes and cook briefly until spices become fragrant. Stir in the beef broth and tomato paste and bring to a boil. Return the lamb and peppers to the casserole. Cover and bake in a preheated 350-degree oven for 1 hour and 15 minutes.

Stir in couscous, raisins, almonds and olives and adjust salt and pepper. Cover and bake an additional 15 minutes, stirring couscous and meat with a fork and adding additional broth as needed so casserole is not dry.

Serves 6.

Old Europe Lamb, Vegetable and Rice Casserole

*T*his is a very hearty dish that needs only a light salad or a dish of sweet-and-sour dilled cucumbers and a loaf of multi-grain bread as accompaniments.

4 tablespoons olive oil, divided
2 tablespoons butter or margarine, divided
2 cups sliced onions
4 cloves garlic, minced
2 cups sliced zucchini
2 tablespoons sweet Hungarian paprika
1/4 teaspoon red pepper flakes
1 teaspoon salt
1/4 teaspoon pepper
2 1/2 pounds boneless leg or shoulder of lamb, trimmed and cut into 2-inch cubes
3 large tomatoes, cut in wedges
2 red or green peppers, seeded and sliced
2 cups coarsely shredded cabbage
1/4 cup chopped parsley
1 teaspoon rosemary, crushed
1 teaspoon marjoram, crushed
1/4 pound green beans, trimmed and cut into short lengths
1 medium eggplant, peeled and diced into 1-inch cubes
3/4 cup raw rice
1 1/2 cups beef broth

In a large skillet over medium heat, melt 1 tablespoon butter and 2 tablespoons oil. Add the onions and saute until limp and golden; add the garlic and saute 2 minutes more. Remove with a slotted spoon and set aside. Add zucchini to the skillet and saute until lightly browned. Remove with a slotted spoon and set aside.

Heat the remaining oil and butter over low heat and add the paprika, pepper flakes, salt and pepper and cook 1 minute. Raise the heat to high, add half the cubed lamb and brown quickly. Remove with a slotted spoon and brown the remaining lamb. Remove and set the meat aside.

Lightly oil a 4-quart casserole and spoon the onions onto the bottom. Layer with half the tomatoes, all the zucchini, half the sliced peppers and all the cabbage. Sprinkle each vegetable lightly with salt and pepper and sprinkle the cabbage with half the parsley, rosemary and marjoram. Next layer the green beans, eggplant, remaining peppers and tomatoes, and again sprinkle each vegetable lightly with salt and pepper. Sprinkle remaining parsley, rosemary and marjoram on top of tomatoes.

Sprinkle the rice on top of the vegetables and cover with the lamb. Pour the broth over all and cover tightly, first with foil and then with the casserole cover. Bake in a preheated 350-degree oven for 1 hour. Baste twice during the cooking time.

Serves 6.

Quick and Easy Scalloped Potatoes with Ham or Corned Beef

We all like to make recipes "from scratch" but, to be realistic, we don't always have the time. Add a fresh green vegetable and a crunchy salad to this quick casserole and you will still have a well-balanced meal.

1 10-ounce can cream of mushroom soup
¾ cup milk
1½ teaspoons dry mustard
½ teaspoon thyme
4 cups peeled and thinly sliced all-purpose potatoes (about 6 medium potatoes)
1 medium onion, halved and thinly sliced
2 cups diced ham or corned beef
1 cup shredded cheddar cheese
2 tablespoons butter

In a small bowl, mix together the soup, milk, dry mustard and thyme.

Butter a 2½-quart casserole and arrange alternate layers of half the potato slices, half the onion slices, half the ham or corned beef and half the soup and milk mixture. Repeat the layers and sprinkle on the shredded cheese and dot with the butter.

Bake, covered, in a preheated 375-degree oven for 1 hour. Uncover and bake an additional 30 minutes.

Serves 6.

Puerco con Vegetales or Pork and Vegetables

For a subtle change of taste we hope you will try the jicama suggested in the recipe. This somewhat sweet, white-fleshed vegetable with the raggedy brown skin is popularly used in Mexican cooking.

2 pounds of boneless pork tenderloin, cut into 1½-inch cubes
3 tablespoons olive oil
1 cup coarsely chopped onions
3 medium carrots, sliced
1 large green pepper, sliced
8 parsley sprigs
1 bay leaf
8 peppercorns
¼ teaspoon fennel seeds
¼ teaspoon freshly grated nutmeg
½ teaspoon cinnamon
½ cup dry white wine
1½ cups chicken broth
1½ pounds jicama, peeled and cut into 1-inch cubes (if unavailable, substitute white potatoes)
2 large tomatoes, halved, seeded and cut into wedges
1 teaspoon salt, or to taste
¼ cup chopped cilantro, for garnish

Heat oil in a 3-quart Dutch oven or large skillet. Add pork, onions, carrots, green pepper, parsley sprigs, bay leaf, peppercorns, fennel seeds, nutmeg and cinnamon and cook, stirring frequently, until the meat loses its pink color. Remove the parsley sprigs.

If using a skillet to brown the meat and vegetables, transfer to a casserole. Add the wine to the skillet and bring to a boil while scraping up the browned bits in the pan. Pour into the casserole and stir in the chicken broth, jicama, tomatoes and salt. Cover and bake in a preheated 350-degree oven for 1½ hours. Stir once during cooking.

Sprinkle with cilantro before serving.

Serves 6.

Pork and Barley with Prunes

This is a hearty dish that would ward off the chill of a blustery winter night. A salad, hot biscuits and a fruit cobbler could round out the menu.

2 pounds lean pork tenderloin, cut into 2-inch cubes
1 cup medium barley
1 pound rutabagas, peeled and cut into 1-inch cubes (turnips or white potatoes can be substituted)
12 pitted prunes, halved
1 teaspoon thyme
½ teaspoon rosemary, crushed
½ teaspoon salt
½ teaspoon pepper
2 tablespoons olive oil
½ cup dry red wine
2½ cups beef broth
¼ cup chopped parsley

Lightly oil a shallow 3-quart casserole dish. Add barley, rutabagas, prunes, thyme, rosemary, salt and pepper and mix together.

Heat olive oil in a large skillet over high heat and brown the meat in 2 batches. Remove with a slotted spoon to the casserole. Add the wine to the skillet and scrape up any browned bits; boil for a minute to burn off the alcohol. Add the beef broth, bring to a boil, then pour over the meat in the casserole. Cover and bake in a preheated 350-degree oven for 1 hour and 45 minutes.

Sprinkle with parsley before serving.

Serves 6.

Dusseldorf Macaroni and Cheese with Kielbasa

A bowl of sweet-and-sour beets would contrast well with this casserole, both visually and in flavor. Of course, a loaf of hand-sliced pumpernickel bread is a must.

8 ounces macaroni or other short tube-shaped pasta, cooked al dente and drained
1-pound ring smoked all-beef kielbasa (Polish sausage), sliced in ½-inch rounds
1 tablespoon olive oil
2 cups coarsely chopped onions
3 tablespoons margarine
3 tablespoons flour
1 cup milk
1 cup chicken broth
2 tablespoons spicy German-style mustard
1 tablespoon brown sugar
1 teaspoon caraway seeds
½ teaspoon thyme
½ teaspoon salt, or more to taste
¼ teaspoon pepper
¾ cup dry bread crumbs
2–3 tablespoons melted margarine
3 cups shredded Swiss cheese

In a large skillet, brown the sausage slices in oil; drain and set aside.

Saute onions in margarine until limp and golden. Stir in the flour and cook 2 minutes. Gradually whisk in the milk and chicken broth, and cook until the sauce thickens. Remove from heat and stir in the mustard, thyme, caraway seeds, brown sugar, salt, pepper and pasta. In a separate bowl, mix remaining margarine with the dry bread crumbs.

Spoon half the pasta mixture into a buttered shallow 3-quart baking dish. Layer half the sausage and half the cheese on top. Repeat and top with bread crumbs. Bake, uncovered, in a preheated 375-degree oven for 30 minutes.

Serves 6.

Italian Casserole with Noodles, Sausage and Zucchini

T his casserole has all the wonderful flavors and ingredients of Italy. A hearty Caesar salad and thick slices of crusty bread will complete your menu.

1 pound mild bulk Italian sausage, or link sausage removed from the casing
1 cup chopped onions
2 cloves garlic, minced
2 tablespoons olive oil
1 tablespoon margarine
3 tablespoons flour
½ teaspoon oregano, crushed
½ teaspoon basil, crushed
½ teaspoon salt
¼ teaspoon freshly ground pepper
1¾ cups milk
¾ cup shredded mozzarella cheese
4 cups cooked wide noodles
1 medium zucchini, scrubbed, halved lengthwise and sliced thinly crosswise
½ cup chopped red or green pepper
1 cup chopped tomatoes
¼ cup chopped parsley
½ cup grated Parmesan cheese

In a large skillet, cook sausage and onions in oil until brown and crumbly; add the garlic for last minute of browning. Remove sausage to a 3-quart casserole, using a slotted spoon, and discard fat in pan.

Heat the oil and margarine in the skillet and stir in flour, oregano and basil and cook for 2 minutes. Gradually stir in the milk with a whisk or wooden spoon and cook until slightly thickened. Stir in mozzarella cheese and cook until melted. Remove from heat and stir in noodles, zucchini, peppers and tomatoes. Pour over the meat in the casserole and mix gently. Taste for salt and pepper. Sprinkle top with parsley and Parmesan cheese. Bake, uncovered, in a 350-degree oven for 30 minutes.

Serves 6.

Baked Sausages and Root Vegetables

Easy, tasty and colorful. What more could you want? Makes a great party dish and is easily expanded to serve a crowd.

2½ pounds best-quality fresh sausage links
12 small red-skinned new potatoes, scrubbed
12 small onions, peeled
8 carrots, about the same size, scraped and cut into equal pieces (or 1-pound package "baby" carrots, already peeled and trimmed)
1 large fennel bulb, cleaned, trimmed and cut into 2-inch pieces
6 small parsnips, peeled and halved
6–8 tablespoons olive oil
2 teaspoons rosemary leaves or Italian seasoning
1 cup chicken or beef broth (or bouillon cube and water)
1 teaspoon salt, or more to taste
¼ teaspoon freshly ground pepper, or more to taste
½ cup finely minced parsley

In a large frying pan, simmer sausages in ½ cup water until water evaporates, then brown sausages in their grease; drain and set aside.

In a 9 x 13-inch shallow baking dish, combine root vegetables with the olive oil, rosemary or Italian seasoning, and salt and pepper to taste. Bring broth to a boil and pour into bottom of the dish; place dish in a preheated 400-degree oven. Bake 1 hour (broth should evaporate). Add sausages and continue baking for 15 more minutes, or until vegetables are tender and sausages are heated through. Place in a large white serving bowl and sprinkle with parsley.

Serves 6.

White Bean and Sausage Casserole

This fast and tasty casserole relies on canned beans and an easily made tomato sauce. An assortment of sausages adds an interesting note, though good-quality "breakfast" sausages are more than acceptable.

2½ pounds assorted fresh sausages, halved or quartered if large
½ cup water
1 large onion, chopped
3 cloves garlic, minced
1 28-ounce can plum tomatoes with juice, chopped
3 tablespoons olive oil
1 stalk celery, chopped fine
1 green pepper, chopped fine
½ teaspoon basil
¼ teaspoon thyme
½ teaspoon salt, or more to taste
¼ teaspoon freshly ground pepper, or more to taste
3 15-ounce cans white beans, rinsed and drained
2 cups fresh bread crumbs
½ cup minced parsley
4 tablespoons butter, melted

In a large frying pan, simmer sausages in ½ cup water until water evaporates, then brown sausages in their own grease; drain on paper towels and set aside.

In a saucepan, saute onion and garlic in the olive oil until lightly brown, then add tomatoes, celery, pepper and seasonings. Simmer, uncovered, for about 30 minutes until sauce has thickened.

Combine sausages, beans, and the tomato sauce and spread in a shallow 9 x 13-inch baking dish. In a bowl, combine the bread crumbs and parsley and sprinkle on casserole. Drizzle the melted butter over casserole and bake in a preheated 375-degree oven about 45 minutes, until bubbly and crusty.

Serves 6.

Sausage and Potato Goulash

S moked sausages of any variety are packed with flavor, and this combination of sausage and potatoes is not unlike a hearty scalloped potato and ham casserole. Serve with chilled chunky applesauce for flavor contrast.

1 tablespoon butter
1 tablespoon olive oil
1½ cups sliced onions
1 cup sliced green pepper
1 tablespoon sweet Hungarian paprika
1½ pounds smoked kielbasa, sliced lengthwise and cut into one-inch pieces
6 cups one-inch-cubed potatoes
1 teaspoon salt
1½ teaspoons marjoram, crushed
1½ cups chicken broth

In a large skillet, heat the butter and oil and saute the onions and green pepper until slightly soft. Remove from the heat and stir in the paprika. Return to a medium heat, add the sausage slices and saute until lightly browned. At this point, either add the remaining ingredients to the skillet and cook on top of the stove or transfer to a 2-quart casserole, add the remaining ingredients and bake in the oven.

To finish in the skillet: Stir in the cubed potatoes, salt, marjoram and chicken broth, cover and simmer over medium-low heat for 30 minutes. Uncover and continue to cook for a few minutes until the sauce is slightly thickened. Spoon into a bowl and serve.

To finish in a casserole: Transfer the onion and sausage mixture to a 2-quart casserole. Stir in the cubed potatoes, salt, marjoram and chicken broth, cover and bake in a preheated 375-degree oven for 30 minutes. Remove the cover and continue to bake for 10 minutes until the sauce thickens slightly.

Serves 6.

Three-Bean and Kielbasa Casserole

America has fallen in love with no-fat, high-protein, high-carbohydrate beans. Here, three different beans are cooked "from scratch" and the Polish sausage, kielbasa, is added for a grand-looking and great-tasting dinner.

2½ pounds kielbasa, smoked or fresh, in one long sausage if possible
1 cup each Great Northern, pinto, and black beans, washed and picked over
Water to cover
3 cloves garlic, minced
1 large onion, diced
1 large carrot, diced
1 stalk celery, diced
16-ounce can plum tomatoes, chopped
Bouquet garni: 2 cloves, 1 bay leaf, 6 peppercorns and ½ teaspoon leaf thyme,
　　all tied together in a cheesecloth bag
Chicken broth or water
½ teaspoon salt, or more to taste
¼ teaspoon freshly ground pepper, or more to taste
2 cups seasoned bread crumbs
½ cup minced parsley for garnish

In a large Dutch oven, cover beans with water and let stand overnight (or follow package directions for a "quick soak"). Drain off any remaining water. Add garlic, vegetables, canned tomatoes and seasonings tied in cheesecloth. Add enough broth or water to cover by an inch. Bring to boil, then simmer, covered, until beans are just tender (about 45 to 60 minutes). Discard cheesecloth bag and add salt and pepper to taste.

Transfer beans and some of their broth (reserve remaining broth) to a 3 to 4-quart round or oval casserole about 2 inches deep. Top with the bread crumbs. Score the sausage link on the diagonal about every 2 inches; do not slice all the way through. Roll sausage into a round or oval and place on beans. Place uncovered casserole in a preheated 375-degree oven and bake about 45 minutes, or until bubbly and crusty. Add more bean broth if mixture becomes too dry. Sprinkle with the chopped parsley.

Serves 6.

Sausage, Rice and Peppers

*H*ot Italian sausage adds all the seasoning necessary to this homey rice bake. Add toasted Italian bread, spread with olive oil and salt and pepper, and a simple green salad for a very satisfying meal.

2 pounds hot Italian bulk sausage, with fennel if possible
3 large peppers, a mixture of green, red and yellow, cut into ½-inch squares
1 large onion, chopped
3 cloves garlic, minced
28-ounce can Italian plum tomatoes, chopped, with their juice
1 cup beef broth
1½ cups raw rice
Additional beef broth, if necessary
½ cup chopped parsley, for garnish

In a large frying pan, saute the sausage until brown, chopping it into small pieces. Remove the sausage to a covered 3-quart casserole and discard all but 3 tablespoons of the sausage fat.

Over high heat, quickly saute the peppers and the onion in the sausage fat for 5 minutes; add the garlic during the last minute of cooking. Scrape into the casserole. Add the tomatoes to the frying pan and cook, uncovered, for 20 minutes. Add the broth and rice, stir and bring to a boil. Add to casserole.

Cover and bake in a preheated 375-degree oven for about 30 minutes until rice is tender. (Add more broth if rice seems too dry.) Sprinkle with the chopped parsley.

Serves 6.

Nina Graybill and Maxine Rapoport are co-authors of THE PASTA SALAD BOOK, COLD SOUPS, HEARTY SALADS and ENJOY! MAKE-AHEAD DINNER PARTY MENUS. They live in Washington, D.C. Ms. Graybill, a literary lawyer, is especially interested in Mediterranean cuisines. For many years, Ms. Rapoport has pursued a wide range of culinary interests, not the least of which is delighting families and friends with her gift for cooking.

Index